The *WIT* and *WISDOM* *of* P·O·L·I·T·I·C·S

The *WIT* and *WISDOM* of P★O★L★I★T★I★C★S

EXPANDED EDITION

Collected, Compiled and Arranged by
CHUCK HENNING

Fulcrum Publishing
Golden, Colorado

Library of Congress Cataloging-in-Publication Data
The Wit and wisdom of politics / collected, compiled, and arranged by Chuck Henning. — Expanded ed.
    p.   cm.
    Includes index.
    ISBN 1-55591-124-2 (pbk.)
    1. Politics, Practical—Quotations, maxims, etc. 2. Quotations, English.
I. Henning, Charles, 1929–
PN6288.P6W57   1992
320—dc20   92–53803
                                                                    CIP

Printed in the United States of America

0   9   8   7   6   5   4   3   2   1

Fulcrum Publishing
350 Indiana Street, Suite 350
Golden, Colorado 80401-5093

To Joe Blake, Sue O'Brien, Dan Buck and Marty Hatcher,
without whose warm encouragement and gentle prodding there
would be no book

Contents

E

F

G

H

I

J

K

L

M

Acknowledgments

In her *Book of Insults*, Nancy McPhee likens the collector of quotations to a parasite "feeding off the labors of others." H.L. Mencken, in compiling his *New Dictionary of Quotations*, refers to his quotation gathering as "literary scavenging." I can now attest to the accuracy of both statements. My sources for accumulating quotations have been numerous, some I frankly don't remember. They are the result of a lifelong habit—jotting down quotable comments on the backs of envelopes, napkins or whatever scrap of paper was handy—only to wonder later about where they came from. They were spotted in books, new and old, magazines, newspapers, movies, radio and television programs and even came from personal observation. Many have been passed along from friends, reporters, government officials and politicians. I have found that once you have a reputation for collecting quotations, others contribute to your cause.

Obviously, quotation books have been important, as a source of information and a source of reference and verification. Over the last twenty years I have gathered a sizable library of quotation books. I regret not being able to list them all because they have become good friends. I'm tempted to paraphrase Will Rogers: "I never met a quotation book I didn't like."

I would like to thank several people for their help with this project. My longtime friend Lee Olson deserves special recognition. In addition to editing and proofreading, he spent countless hours tracking down the information in the authors' index. I must express my appreciation to Fulcrum, Inc., especially publisher Bob Baron, who, I am happy to report, shares my predilection for the apt quotation. I should not forget Bob's staff: Betsy Armstrong, Cara Smedley, Susan Harlow and Jay Staten. Their patience, industry, enthusiasm and good humor have been invaluable. Joe Blake, Sue O'Brien, Dan Buck and Marty Hatcher also deserve recognition. Without their quiet encouragement and gentle prodding, this project would still be but lines in my speeches and pages in my notebooks. Finally, I am aware of such things as errors, mistaken attributions and inadvertent invasions of copyright. Corrections, remonstrances and the like, if sent to me in care of Fulcrum, Inc., will be gratefully received. As for readers who find their favorite quotation missing, it's not because I didn't try: the supply of material simply exceeded the space. I hope this situation will be remedied at some future date with Son (or Daughter) of *Wit and Wisdom*.

Introduction

Writing in 1580, a French essayist put his pen precisely on the motives that were to inspire my own love affair with quotations some three centuries later.

I quote others to better express myself.

Michel de Montaigne

But the effort "to better express myself " was only the first step in my journey. The second step came when I realized that, although I wasn't particularly witty myself, I was able to trade on the wit of others.

Next to being witty yourself, the best thing is being able to quote others.

Christian N. Bovee

Further I observed that politics has become far too pompous and that politicians take themselves far too seriously.

Nobody has ever said anything on behalf of politicians so sharp and true as many intelligent men have said against them.

Ferdinand Lundberg

And so I set out to collect the wit and humor of politics. My intention was to help the system function better (and to prick a few political egos in the process). But the compendium of wit and humor soon took on an added dimension: I found myself trying to cover political wisdom as well.

The wisdom of the wise and the experience of the ages are perpetuated by quotations.

Benjamin Disraeli

By now I'm able to find borrowed words to fit virtually every situation. As an author, I can apologize for the length of this volume.

CHUCK HENNING

Most anthologists...of quotations are like those who eat cherries...first picking the best ones and winding up by eating everything.

Nicholas Chamfort

As an anthologist, I can explain my policies on selection.

About the most originality that any writer can hope to achieve is to steal with good judgment.

Josh Billings

As a borrower, I can explain my philosophy on attribution.

When you take stuff from one writer, it's plagiarism; but when you take it from many writers, it's research.

Wilson Mizner

What follows represents my research. It is both a labor of love and a reminder to those involved in our system of government and politics that, while the process will never work perfectly, it will be better served if all involved learn to take themselves less seriously.

Of all the quotations in my collection, I have one personal favorite:

I am but a gatherer and disposer of other men's stuff.

Sir Henry Wotton

Were I a plagiarist, my own epitaph then might read:

I was but a gatherer and disposer of other men's and women's stuff.

Chuck Henning

A

ABILITY

It is a great ability to be able to conceal one's ability.

La Rochefoucauld

In the last analysis, ability is commonly found to consist mainly in a high degree of solemnity.

Ambrose Bierce

Ability is of little account without opportunity.

Napoleon Bonaparte

The ablest man I ever met is the man you think you are.

Franklin D. Roosevelt

Natural ability without education has more often raised a man to glory and virtue than education without natural ability.

Cicero

They are able because they think they are able.

Virgil

Intelligence is quickness to apprehend as distinct from ability, which is capacity to act wisely on the thing apprehended.

Alfred North Whitehead

The winds and waves are always on the side of the ablest navigator.

Edward Gibbon

ACCEPTANCE SPEECHES

One candidate has notified us that his acceptance speech will be very long. The other candidate says that his will be very short. I wonder why one of them don't announce that his will be very good?

Will Rogers

If we got one-tenth of what was promised to us in these acceptance speeches there wouldn't be any inducement to go to heaven.

Will Rogers

This election is not about ideology: it's about competence.

Michael Dukakis

Acceptance speech. Designed to please everyone, offend no one and get the delegates back to the bar before it closes.

B.C. comic strip

ACCOMPLISHMENT

The world is divided into people who do things—and people who get the credit.

Dwight Morrow

There is nothing more disappointing than failing to accomplish a thing, unless it is to see somebody else accomplish it.

Henry S. Haskins

Every man who is high up loves to think he has done it all himself; and his wife smiles, and lets it go at that.

Sir James M. Barrie

It is not enough to aim, you must hit.

Italian proverb

Nothing great was ever achieved without great men, and men are great only if they are determined to be so.

Charles de Gaulle

It's the people who are a little eccentric who get things done.

Ed Koch

Perhaps one of the most important accomplishments of my administration has been minding my own business.

Calvin Coolidge

ADMIRATION

I admire him [Cecil Rhodes], I frankly confess it; and when his time comes, I shall buy a piece of the rope for a keepsake.

Mark Twain

Admiration: our polite recognition of another's resemblance to ourselves.

Ambrose Bierce

Things not understood are admired.

Thomas Fuller, M.D.

ADVERSARIES

Treating your adversary with respect is giving him an advantage to which he is not entitled.

Samuel Johnson

I respect only those who resist me, but I cannot tolerate them.

Charles de Gaulle

I have no permanent enemies—only people I have yet to persuade.

Richard Lamm

ADVERTISING

You can fool all the people all the time if the advertising is right and the budget is big enough.

Joseph Levine

The professional politician can sympathize with the professional advertiser. Both must resign themselves to a low public estimation of their veracity and sincerity.

Enoch Powell

Advertising men and politicians are dangerous if they are separated. Together they are diabolical.

Philip Adams

Advertising is the rattling of a stick inside a swill bucket.

George Orwell (attr.)

Advertising may be described as the science of arresting human intelligence long enough to get money from it.

Stephen Leacock

A good ad should be like a good sermon: It must not only comfort the afflicted—it also must afflict the comfortable.

Bernice Fitz-Gibbon

Advertising is a racket . . . its constructive contribution to humanity is exactly minus zero.

F. Scott Fitzgerald

ADVICE

In giving advice I advise you, be short.

Horace

If someone gives you so-called good advice, do the opposite; you can be sure it will be the right thing nine out of ten times.

Anselm Feuerbach

It is wrong to follow the advice of an adversary; nevertheless it is right to hear it, that you may do the contrary; and this is the essence of good policy.

Sadi

Advice is judged by results, not by intentions.

Cicero

In those days he was wiser than he is now; he used frequently to take my advice.

Winston S. Churchill

I always pass on good advice. It is the only thing to do with it. It is never any use to oneself.

Oscar Wilde

I have found the best way to give advice to your children is to find out what they want and then advise them to do it.

Harry S. Truman

Advice is like castor oil, easy enough to give but dreadfully uneasy to take.

Josh Billings

"Be yourself" is about the worst advice you can give some people.

Tom Masson

He had only one vanity; he thought he could give advice better than any other person.

Mark Twain

When we ask advice, we are usually looking for an accomplice.

Marquis de La Grange

Old men are fond of giving bad advice to console themselves for being no longer in a position to give bad examples.

La Rochefoucauld

When everything is going badly and you are trying to make up your mind, look toward the heights, no complications there.

Charles de Gaulle

THE WIT AND WISDOM OF POLITICS

If you start to take Vienna—take Vienna.

Napoleon Bonaparte

Never speak of yourself to others; make them talk about themselves instead; therein lies the whole art of pleasing. Everyone knows it and everyone forgets it.

Edmond and Jules de Goncourt

If you want to get rid of somebody, just tell 'em something for their own good.

Frank McKinney Hubbard

Always do right; this will gratify some people and astonish the rest.

Mark Twain

Senators are a prolific source of advice, and most of it is bad.

Dean Acheson

If you can't convince them confuse them.

Harry S. Truman

Don't jump on a man unless he's down.

Finley Peter Dunne

Don't get mad, get even.

Joseph P. Kennedy (attr.)

Never forget, rarely forgive.

Ed Koch

Keep cool: it will be all one a hundred years hence.

Ralph Waldo Emerson

Never eat at a place called Mom's. Never play cards with a man called Doc. And never lie down with a woman who's got more troubles than you.

Nelson Algren

A man should be careful never to tell tales of himself to his own disadvantage. People may be amused and laugh at the time, but they will be remembered and brought against him upon some subsequent occasion.

Samuel Johnson

If a man loves to give advice, it is a sure sign that he himself wants it.

George Savile

5

CHUCK HENNING

When a man seeks your advice he generally wants your praise.
Lord Chesterfield

Never apologize. Never explain. Never retract.
Joseph Chamberlain

Be frank and explicit. That is the right line to take, when you wish to conceal your own mind and to confuse the minds of others.
Benjamin Disraeli

If you must hold yourself up to your children as an object lesson, hold yourself up as a warning and not as an example.
George Bernard Shaw

And do as adversaries do in law. Strive mightily, but eat and drink as friends.
William Shakespeare

Quiet, calm deliberation disentangles every knot.
W.S. Gilbert

Perhaps one of the only positive pieces of advice that I was ever given was that supplied by an old courtier, who observed: only two rules really count. Never miss an opportunity to relieve yourself; never miss a chance to sit down and rest your feet.
Duke of Windsor

Be nice to people on the way up, because you'll meet them on your way down.
Wilson Mizner

I always looked at everything from the point of view of what I ought to do, rarely from what I wanted to do.
Anna Eleanor Roosevelt

I never got in trouble for what I never said.
Calvin Coolidge

All you need to know is this. You can never go wrong voting for a bill that fails, or against a bill that passes.
Robert Dole

AGREEMENT
My idea of an agreeable person is a person who agrees with me.
Benjamin Disraeli

When people agree with me, I always feel that I must be wrong.

Oscar Wilde

When you say that you agree to a thing in principle, you mean that you have not the slightest intention of carrying it out in practice.

Otto von Bismarck

It is by universal misunderstanding that all agree. For if, by ill luck, people understood each other, they would never agree.

Charles Baudelaire

We agree completely on everything, including the fact we don't see eye to eye.

Henry Kissinger
Golda Meir

AMBITION

You really have to be careful of politicians who have no further ambitions: they may run for the Presidency.

Eugene McCarthy

I have no ambitions beyond my present stepping stone.

Philip Sorenson

Most people would succeed in small things if they were not troubled by great ambitions.

Henry Wadsworth Longfellow

The greatest evil which fortune can inflict on men is to endow them with small talents and great ambition.

Vauvenargues

Everybody sets out to do something, and everybody does something, but no one does what he sets out to do.

George Moore

Every normal man must be tempted at times, to spit on his hands, hoist the black flag, and begin slitting throats.

H.L. Mencken

It's ambition that gets you here [Congress]. It's paranoia that keeps you here.

Mike Synar

AMERICA

It has often been asked what this nation stands for, and the question is easy—too much.

Anonymous

The United States is a country of quiet majorities and vociferous minorities.

Anonymous

I don't know much about Americanism, but it's a damned good word with which to carry an election.

Warren G. Harding

Divine Providence has under its special protection children, idiots and the United States of America.

Lord James Bryce

America is a large friendly dog in a small room. Every time it wags its tail it knocks over a chair.

Arnold Toynbee

The Italian author Guido Piovene once compared the United States to a huge digestive system. All kinds of abrasives can be introduced into it. But like the oyster it has an infinite capacity to secrete social gastric juices which transform the rough stones of dissent into smooth pearls of conformity. If this is true, or even half true, American revolutionists face an impossible task.

Denis Goulet

In our society, humility is not our strong suit. We almost violently reject the prospect of being a loser. Yet we must be prepared to admit that we can be wrong. If we are so insecure as to feel we are worthless if we make a mistake, and thus cannot manfully acknowledge our mistakes, we are in deep trouble. One of the ills of this nation is the insecurity of so many people who have to believe we are always right, that we have never erred—that we are infallible. This is a delusion.

Walter Menninger

We must all learn to live together as Brothers. Or we will all perish together as fools.

Martin Luther King, Jr.

I hear that melting pot stuff a lot and all I can say is that we haven't melted.

Jesse Jackson

The three-martini lunch is the epitome of American efficiency. Where else can you get an earful, a bellyful, and a snootful at the same time.

Gerald Ford

Each generation of Americans has to face circumstances not of its own choosing, by which its character is measured and its spirit is tested.

James Earl Carter, Jr.

APATHY

We do not say that a man who takes no interest in politics is a man who minds his own business; we say that he has no business here at all.

Pericles

The tyranny of a prince in an oligarchy is not so dangerous to the public welfare as the apathy of a citizen in a democracy.

Charles de Montesquieu

Good laws lead to the making of better ones; bad ones bring about worse. As soon as any man says of the affairs of State: "What does it matter to me?" the State may be given up for lost.

Jean-Jacques Rousseau

The only thing necessary for the triumph of evil is for good men to do nothing.

Edmund Burke

The death of democracy is not likely to be an assassination from ambush. It will be a slow extinction from apathy, indifference and undernourishment.

Robert M. Hutchins

Bad officials are elected by good citizens who do not vote.

George Jean Nathan

It's just got so that 90 percent of the people in this country don't give a damn. Politics ain't worrying this country one tenth as much as parking space.

Will Rogers

APPEARANCE

If I've learned anything in my seventy years, it's that nothing's as good or as bad as it appears.

Bushrod H. Campbell

For the great majority of mankind are satisfied with appearances, as though they were realities, and are often more influenced by the things that seem than those that are.

Niccolò Machiavelli

APPOINTMENTS

Every time I fill a vacant office I make ten malcontents and one ingrate.

Louis XIV

If due participation of office is a matter of right, how are vacancies to be obtained? Those by death are few; by resignation, none.

Thomas Jefferson

No duty the Executive had to perform was so trying as trying to put the right man in the right place.

Thomas Jefferson

I shall not, whilst I have the honor to administer the government, bring a man into any office of consequence knowingly, whose political tenets are adverse to the measures, which the general government are pursuing; for this, in my opinion, would be a sort of political suicide.

George Washington

Senator, I ordinarily make good appointments. I think I have made very few mistakes. But when I make a mistake, it's a beaut.

Fiorello H. La Guardia

Everybody wants to be Secretary of State.

John F. Kennedy

Take from the United States, the appointment of postmasters and let the towns elect them, and you deprive the Federal Government of half a million defenders.

Ralph Waldo Emerson

In American politics, a person who having failed to secure an office from the people is given one by the Administration on condition that he leave the country.

Ambrose Bierce

No man who ever held the office of President would congratulate a friend on obtaining it. He will make one man ungrateful and a hundred men his enemies for every office he can bestow.

John Adams

Patronage: governmental appointments made so as to increase political strength.

William Safire

Politics makes strange postmasters.

Frank McKinney Hubbard

Patronage is hard business, abounding in bleak moments for its transactors.

Louis Koenig

[Patronage] . . . an occupational hazard of democracy.

Martin and Susan Tolchin

One of the principal qualifications for a political job is that the applicant know nothing much about what he is expected to do.

Terry M. Townsend

Our present mayor has the distinction of appointing more saloon keepers and bartenders to public office than any previous mayor.

Unidentified clergyman
on Boston Mayor John "Honey Fitz" Fitzgerald

I acknowledge that you can't keep an organization together without patronage. Men ain't in politics for nothin'. They want to get somethin' out of it.

George Washington Plunkitt

I didn't vote for you, I didn't even think of voting for you and I probably won't next time.

Robert Strauss

You are the first person to say that to me since I've been sitting behind this desk. That's why I want you for the job.

George Bush

APPROPRIATIONS

He who has his thumb on the purse has the power.

Otto von Bismarck

An appropriation was a tangible thing, if you got hold of it, and it made little difference what it was appropriated for, so long as you got hold of it.

Mark Twain

Everyone is always in favor of general economy and particular expenditure.

Sir Anthony Eden

All were agreed upon one point, however: if Congress would make a sufficient appropriation, a colossal benefit would result.

Mark Twain

They are always wanting the government to spend the taxpayers' money to build something. Every congressman wants to get an appropriation to dam up his client's little stream with federal funds. If the politicians have their way, there won't be a foot of water in this country that's not standing above a dam.

Will Rogers

One million dollars: A minor item in your appropriation, a mere pittance for those who deserve much more. One million dollars: In their bill, another raid on the Treasury, a flagrant example of squandering public funds.

Merriman Smith

A billion here, a billion there and pretty soon you're talking about real money.

Everett McKinley Dirksen

We know in our hearts that we are in the world for keeps, yet we are still tackling twenty-year problems with five-year plans staffed by two-year personnel working with one-year appropriations. It's simply not good enough.

Harlan Cleveland

ARGUMENTS

Discussion is an exchange of knowledge; argument is an exchange of ignorance.

Robert Quillen

It is not necessary to understand things in order to argue about them.
Pierre de Beaumarchais

He who frames the argument often wins it.

George Will

I dislike arguments of any kind. They are always vulgar, and often convincing.

Oscar Wilde

I never make the mistake of arguing with people for whose opinions I have no respect.

Edward Gibbon

The most savage controversies are those about matters as to which there is no good evidence either way.

Bertrand Russell

It is difficult to win an argument when your opponent is unencumbered with a knowledge of the facts.

Anonymous

Silence is one of the hardest things to refute.

Josh Billings

It is difficult to be emphatic when no one is emphatic on the other side.
Charles Dudley Warner

I always get the better when I argue alone.

Oliver Goldsmith

You raise your voice when you should reinforce your argument.
Samuel Johnson

It is a difficult matter, my fellow citizens, to argue with the belly, since it has no ears.

Cato

When you have no basis for an argument, abuse the plaintiff.
Cicero

Mr. Lloyd George . . . spoke for a hundred and seventeen minutes, in which period he was detected only once in the use of an argument.
Arnold Bennett

I always cheer up immensely if an attack is particularly wounding because I think well if they attack me personally, it means they have not a single political argument left.

Margaret Thatcher

ARROGANCE
I'm not arrogant. I just believe there's no human problem that couldn't be solved—if people would simply do as I tell 'em.
Donald Regan

Early in life I had a chance to choose between honest arrogance and hypocritical humility. I chose honest arrogance and have seen no occasion to change.

Frank Lloyd Wright

BALLOTS

Ballots are the rightful and peaceful successors to bullets.

Abraham Lincoln

The ballot is stronger than the bullet.

Abraham Lincoln

Anyone can win, unless there happens to be a second entry.

George Ade

BIGOTS

Bigot, n.
One who is obstinately and zealously attached to an opinion that you do not entertain.

Ambrose Bierce

Wisdom never has made a bigot, but learning has.

Josh Billings

It is only the "educated" man, especially the literary man, who knows how to be a bigot . . .

George Orwell

The people who are most bigoted are the people who have no convictions at all.

G.K. Chesterton

A bigot delights in public ridicule, for he begins to think he is a martyr.

Sydney Smith

BLAME

It isn't whether you win or lose but how you place the blame.

Chuck Howe

Then there were the immortal words of French General Joseph Joffre when he was asked who won the battle of the Marne:

I don't know who won it, but if we had lost I know who would have been blamed.

The accusations really say more about the condition of the accusers than that of the accused.

Roderick MacLeish

BUDGET

Look at the president. He started in with the idea of a balanced budget, and said that was what he would hold out for. But look at the thing now. Poor president, he tried but couldn't do it by persuasion and he can't do it by law. So he may just have to give it up and say: "Boys, I have tried but I guess it's back to the old ways of an unbalanced budget."

Will Rogers

The budget is a mythical beanbag. Congress votes mythical beans into it, and then tries to reach in and pull real beans out.

Will Rogers

The longer something hangs around here, it gets stale. People start reading it.

Robert Dole

I couldn't help thinking that, if the definition of a good budget proposal is to distribute dissatisfaction, ours is a real winner.

Ronald Reagan

As one of the senators here said, "You'll find that all of us individually have the courage to make a tough decision. The problem is to find twenty-five senators who have the courage simultaneously."

Robert Kerrey

Any budget director who can't make $100 million appear and disappear isn't worth his salt.
Unidentified budget director for New York Governor Nelson Rockefeller

In national affairs a million is only a drop in the budget.

Burton Rascoe

In government the budget is the message.

I.F. Stone

It's a terribly hard job to spend a billion dollars and get your money's worth.

George Humphrey

Those who work out our federal budget
Have a policy—really a honey—
We shall live on our national income,
Even if we must borrow the money.

Leverett Lyon

The final budget . . . was a compromise in the sense that being bitten in half by a shark is a compromise with being swallowed whole.

P.J. O'Rourke

BUREAUCRACY

The nearest thing to immortality in this world.

Hugh Johnson

If there's anything a public servant hates to do it's something for the public.

Frank McKinney Hubbard

The only good bureaucrat is one with a pistol at his head. Put it in his hand and it's goodbye to the Bill of Rights.

H.L. Mencken

Bureaucracies are designed to perform public business. But as soon as a bureaucracy is established, it develops an autonomous spiritual life and comes to regard the public as its enemy.

Brooks Atkinson

The perfect bureaucrat everywhere is the man who manages to make no decisions and escape all responsibility.

Brooks Atkinson

An efficient bureaucracy is the greatest threat to liberty.

Eugene McCarthy

Civilization declines in relation to the increase in bureaucracy.

Victor Yannacone

Bureaucracy defends the status quo long past the time when the quo has lost its status.

Laurence J. Peter

THE WIT AND WISDOM OF POLITICS

A bureaucrat is a Democrat who holds some office that a Republican wants.

Alben W. Barkley

Bureaucrat: A person who proceeds in a straight line from an unknown assumption to a foreign conclusion.

Albert Hawkes

Bureaucratic function is sustained by fear of failure as the church was once supported by fear of damnation.

Richard N. Goodwin

A bureaucracy is a continuing congregation of people who must act more or less as one.

John K. Galbraith

[Dealing with bureaucracy] is like trying to nail jelly to the wall.

John F. Kennedy

Working with the government is sometimes like spinning your wheels in the sand.

Louis Thiess

Guidelines for Bureaucrats: (1) When in charge ponder. (2) When in trouble delegate. (3) When in doubt mumble.

James H. Boren

A memorandum is written not to inform the reader but to protect the writer.

Dean Acheson

I have learned that the surest form of bureaucratic birth control when confronted by a fertile idea is to direct your colleague to put it in a memo.

Arnold R. Weber

The proposal is frequently made that the government ought to assume the risks that are "too great for private industry." This means that bureaucrats should be permitted to take risks with the taxpayers' money that no one is willing to take with his own.

Henry Hazlitt

I honestly believe that drink is the greatest curse of the day, except, of course, civil service, and that it has driven more young men to ruin than anything except civil service examinations.

George Washington Plunkitt

[Bureaucracy]. A giant mechanism operated by pygmies.

Honoré de Balzac

There is no passion like that of a functionary for his function.

Georges Clemenceau

Fear of criticism and freedom of thought by combining together with bureaucracy quite often produce ridiculous forms.

Aleksandra Kollontai

A government of statesmen or of clerks? Of Humbug or of Humdrum?

Benjamin Disraeli

A difficulty for every solution.

Lord Samuel (attr.)

A politician or a civil servant is still to me an arrogant fool until he is proved otherwise.

Neville Shute

The worst thing that can be said about a civil servant is that he is emotional.

Richard Adams

He [Inland Revenue official] looked like a cardboard hangman. Poisoned ink, paper clip stilettos and suffocation by forms.

Anthony Carson

A civil servant is a faceless mortal riding like a flea on the back of the dog, Legislation.

Anonymous

You don't need brains to be Minister of Transport because the civil servants have them.

Ernest Marples

[The faults of bureaucracy] clearly arise from the difficulty of controlling experts in any department where action depends upon special knowledge which as a rule they alone possess, and where mistakes of innovation may entail serious consequences. The size of the modern State in fact tends to make its government an oligarchy of specialists, whose routine is disturbed by the occasional irruption of the benevolent amateur.

Harold J. Laski

Bureaucracy is the antithesis of democracy.

Joseph Grimond

Civil servants, like Americans, want to be loved. But one cannot love bureaucratic power. Only submit to it, fear it or hate it. Civil servants are the "they" in our society.

Douglas Houghton

Civil servants—men who write minutes, make professional assessments, who are never attacked face to face, who dwell in the Sargasso Sea of the Civil Service and who love the seaweed that conceals them.

William Connor

An official man is always an official man, and he has a wild belief in the value of reports.

Sir Arthur Helps

If you're going to sin, sin against God, not the bureaucracy. God will forgive you but the bureaucracy won't.

Hyman G. Rickover

BUSINESS

The business of government is to keep the government out of business—that is, unless business needs government aid.

Will Rogers

I niver knew a pollytician to go wrong until he's been contaminated by contact with a business man.

Finley Peter Dunne

Government in the U.S. today is a senior partner in every business in the country.

Norman Cousins

You never expected justice from a company did you? They have neither a soul to lose, nor a body to kick.

Sydney Smith

Don't steal; thou'lt never thus compete successfully in business. Cheat.
Ambrose Bierce

When government enters the field of business with great resources, it has a tendency to extravagance and inefficiency, but, having the power to crush all competitors, likewise closes the door of opportunity and results in monopoly.

Calvin Coolidge

The difficulty with businessmen entering politics, after they've had a successful business career, is that they want to start at the top.

Harry S. Truman

We do many things at the federal level that would be considered dishonest and illegal if done in the private sector.

Donald Regan

Anything the private sector can do, the government can do it worse.

Dixie Lee Ray

CAMPAIGNS

A most wretched custom is our electioneering and scrambling for office.

Cicero

Political campaigns are designedly made into emotional orgies which endeavor to distract attention from the real issues involved, and they actually paralyze what slight powers of cerebration man can normally muster.

James Harvey Robinson

Football strategy does not originate in a scrimmage: it is useless to expect solutions in a political campaign.

Walter Lippmann

The hardest thing about any political campaign is how to win without proving that you are unworthy of winning.

Adlai Stevenson

You learn more about yourself while campaigning for just one week than in six months spent with a psychoanalyst.

Adlai Stevenson

I guess the truth can hurt you worse in an election than about anything that could happen to you.

Will Rogers

The campaign ends Tuesday, but it will take two generations to sweep up the dirt.

Will Rogers

THE WIT AND WISDOM OF POLITICS

A national campaign is better than the best circus ever heard of, with a mass baptism and a couple of hangings thrown in. It is better, even, than war.

H.L. Mencken

It is not a smear, if you please, if you point out the record of your opponent.

Murray Chotiner

Although I myself do not drink, I always make a point of shaking hands with bartenders whenever I come across them, because their recommendations, voiced at that moment when men's minds are highly receptive to ideas, carry much weight in a community.

Joseph William Martin

For a candidate to spend millions of dollars during the primaries to win a job that pays only $100,000 a year doesn't bode well for the citizens' hopes of electing a man to this high office whose knowledge of economics will balance our national budget.

Goodman Ace

I don't want to spend the next two years in Holiday Inns.

Walter Mondale

...The seeds of political success are sown far in advance of any election day.... It is the sum total of the little things that happen which leads to eventual victory at the polls.

J. Howard McGrath

Charge and warn, never offer a concrete solution.

Franz Josef Strauss

I do not approve of "front porch" campaigns. I never liked to see any man elected to office who did not go out and meet the people in person and work for their votes.

Harry S. Truman

In most of my campaigns, I find it best not to mention my opponent by name because, by doing so, it just gives him a chance to get into the headlines.

Harry S. Truman

It isn't important who is ahead at one time or another in either an election or a horse race. It's the horse that comes in first at the finish that counts.

Harry S. Truman

21

A healthy democratic political system rests on the ability of the electorate to know, understand and judge the attitudes, characteristics, opinions and qualifications of candidates for public office. Clearly, political campaigns are essential to democracy.

John F. Kennedy

But as we all know, the truth is a frequent casualty in the heat of an election campaign.

Thomas P. O'Neill

Once when Disraeli was canvassing for votes door to door, a woman opened the door, Disraeli paused and then explaining his pause, exclaimed: "I was overcome by the resemblance to my sainted mother—and she was a very beautiful woman."

George Will

You campaign in poetry, you govern in prose.

Mario Cuomo

When I was campaigning for re-election to my second term in Congress, I spoke in a rural Indiana community, giving my views and asking for . . . support. The group was an appreciative and responsive one, and after my remarks I was approached by an enthusiastic listener. He expressed a few thoughts to me and finished by saying, "Son, I like what you say, and I believe I'll vote for you. By golly, anything will be better than the Congressman we have now."

Richard L. Roudebush

We were told our campaign wasn't sufficiently slick. We regard that as a compliment.

Margaret Thatcher

CANDIDATES

We'd all like t' vote for th' best man, but he's never a candidate.
Frank McKinney Hubbard

The election isn't very far off when a candidate can recognize you across the street.
Frank McKinney Hubbard

The best thing about this group of candidates is that only one of them can win.
Will Rogers

THE WIT AND WISDOM OF POLITICS

The saddest life is that of a political aspirant under democracy. His failure is ignominious and his success is disgraceful.

H.L. Mencken

A candidate for office can have no greater advantage than muddled syntax; no greater liability than a command of the language.

Marya Mannes

He who slings mud generally loses ground.

Adlai Stevenson

A Presidential candidate has to shave twice a day—and I don't like that.

Adlai Stevenson

The idea that you can merchandise candidates for high office like breakfast cereal—that you can gather votes like box tops—is, I think, the ultimate indignity to the democratic process.

Adlai Stevenson

Offices are as acceptable here as elsewhere, and whenever a man has cast a longing eye on them, a rottenness begins in his conduct.

Thomas Jefferson

Never, never, you must never . . . remind a man at work on a political job that he may be president. It almost always kills him politically. He loses his nerve; he can't do his work; he gives up the very traits that are making him a possibility.

Theodore Roosevelt

This office-seeking is a disease. It is even catching.

Grover Cleveland

In 1980, as the presidential campaign was approaching, Arizona Congressman Mo Udall, who had run previously, was approached by the media and asked if he might again get into the contest. He replied:

Only on three conditions: If a star rises in the east, if three men on camels ride up to my door demanding that I run and if their names are Carter, Mondale and Kennedy.

Running for the Third Congressional District is my second priority. My first priority is swimming naked through a pool of piranhas.

Martin Hatcher

... It is not the fault of the candidates. Many of them are honest, courageous, and sincere, with a real desire for public service. The chief trouble is the utter impossibility of appealing squarely to the intelligence of the voters and getting an impartial verdict on merit. It simply cannot be done. The voters are not like that. Notoriously, most of them vote from prejudice.

Frank R. Kent

The first thing you do when you want to get elected is to prostitute yourself. You show me a man with courage and conviction and I'll show you a loser.

Ray Kroc

If you're not big enough to lose, you're not big enough to win.

Walter Reuther

It's dangerous for a national candidate to say things that people might remember.

Eugene McCarthy

A candidate running for Congress hired two assistants: one to dig up the facts and the other to bury them.

Anonymous

It's par for the course trying to fool the people but it's downright dangerous when you start fooling yourself.

Gore Vidal

Because he's a bastard doesn't mean he wouldn't make a good candidate. Or even a good President.

Gore Vidal

If you have a weak candidate and a weak platform, wrap yourself up in the American flag and talk about the Constitution.

Matt Quay

The best character that can be given any candidate is that he is so rich he does not need to steal.

New York Herald Tribune
editorial in the 1840s

You can't beat somebody with nobody.

Joseph G. Cannon

Kelley's Law. Last guys don't finish nice.

Stanley Kelley

There are hardly two creatures of a more differing Species than the same man, when he is pretending to a Place, and when he is in possession of it.

George Savile

I am sure that many political candidates are defeated because the public has been given an opportunity to see what they look like. The next great political victory will be achieved by the party that is smart enough to have nobody heading the ticket.

Groucho Marx

You know, the only thing the American people like less than a dirty fighter is someone who won't fight.

Tom Harkin

I know as a candidate I should kiss your ass, but I haven't learned to do that with equanimity yet.

John Silber

We noncandidates don't have to do what the candidates do—talk about huge issues in thirty seconds in a field somewhere, trying to make sure cows don't urinate on our shoes.

Mario Cuomo

I have no plans and no plans to have plans.

Mario Cuomo

I'm not agonizing. I'm not delaying. Nor am I struggling over the decision. I'm struggling over the facts. Once I get all of the facts, I'll make the decision . . . in less than three hours.

Mario Cuomo

Mario Cuomo's public service campaign: A mind is a terrible thing to make up.

Jay Leno

I thought he was going to run. Then I didn't think he was going to run. Then I did. Now I don't care.

Bob Beckel
on Mario Cuomo

CAUCUSES

Caucus: A political term that is truly American in origin. It traces its roots to an Algonquin Indian word meaning "counselor" or "advisor." The initial appearance of the word "caucus" was in John Adams' diary in February 1753:

Thursday the caucus club meets . . . in the garret of Tom Dawes, the adjutant of the Boston regiment.

Adams went on to describe what happened at a caucus:

There they smoke tobacco till you cannot see from one end of the garret to the other. There they drink flip, I suppose, and there they choose a moderator—who puts questions to the vote regularly; and selectmen, assessors, wardens and representatives are regularly chosen before they are chosen by the town.

If he had attended the caucus on creation, he would have stayed loyal to chaos.

Anonymous
on Joe Cannon

I think caucuses are a waste of time. You lose more votes than you gain.
Sam Rayburn

The difference between a caucus and a cactus is that a cactus has the pricks on the outside.

Morris Udall (attr.)

CAUSES

We were always subject to this pressure from the cause people. We reacted to every threat from women, or militants, or college groups. If I had to do it all over again, I'd learn to tell them to go to hell.
Frank Mankiewicz

It is characteristic of all movements and crusades that the psychopathic element rises to the top.

Robert Lindner

The whole method of judging a cause by the actions and words of the worst type of person you can find among its supporters is too cheap—I believe I've done it sometime in politics, but I vow I won't anymore—it's tempting because it's so easy.

C.E. Montague

Nothing fails like success; nothing is so defeated as yesterday's triumphant cause.

Phyllis McGinley

We are all ready to be savage in some cause. The difference between a good man and a bad one is the choice of the cause.

William James

A bad cause will ever be supported by bad means and bad men.

Thomas Paine

In a just cause the weak will beat the strong.

Sophocles

If a cause be good, the most violent attack of its enemies will not injure it so much as an injudicious defense by its friends.

Charles Caleb Colton

Those whose cause is just will never lack good arguments.

Euripides

He that hath the worst cause makes the most noise.

Thomas Fuller, D.D.

Obstinacy in a bad cause is but constancy in a good.

Sir Thomas Browne

The best cause requires a good pleader.

Dutch proverb

A just cause is not ruined by a few mistakes.

Fyodor Dostoevsky

We can be satisfied with moderate confidence in ourselves and with a moderately good opinion of ourselves, but the faith we have in a holy cause has to be extravagant and uncompromising.

Eric Hoffer

Faith in a holy cause is to a considerable extent a substitute for the lost faith in ourselves.

Eric Hoffer

I hate the idea of causes, and if I had to choose between betraying my country and betraying my friend, I hope I should have the guts to betray my country.

E.M. Forster

CENSURE

Censure is a tax a man pays to the public for being eminent.

Jonathan Swift

It is harder to avoid censure than to gain applause; for this may be done by one great or wise action in an age. But to escape censure a man must pass his whole life without saying or doing one ill or foolish thing.

David Hume

They'll [the House Un-American Activities Committee] nail anyone who ever scratched his ass during the National Anthem.

Humphrey Bogart

CHANCE

Although men flatter themselves with their great actions, they are usually the result of chance and not of design.

La Rochefoucauld

Chance is a word void of sense; nothing can exist without a cause.

Voltaire

Chance rules men and not men chances.

Herodotus

Chance never helps those who do not help themselves.

Sophocles

Chance is always powerful; let your hook always be cast. In a pool where you least expect it there will be a fish.

Ovid

I returned and saw under the sun, that the race is not to the swift, nor the battle to the strong, neither yet bread to the wise, nor yet riches to men of understanding, nor yet favor to men of skill; but time and chance happeneth to them all.

Ecclesiastes 9:11

A fool must now and then be right by chance.

William Cowper

Chance happens to all, but to turn chance to account is the gift of few.

Edward Bulwer-Lytton

He that leaveth nothing to Chance will do few things ill, but he will do very few things.

George Savile

I do not believe such a quality as chance exists. Every incident that happens must be a link in a chain.

Benjamin Disraeli

Things do not happen in this world—they are brought about.

Will Hays

It is not Justice the servant of men, but accident, hazard, Fortune—the ally of patient Time—that holds an even and scrupulous balance.

Joseph Conrad

Great politicians owe their reputation, if not to pure chance, then to circumstances at least which they themselves could not foresee.

Otto von Bismarck

Every possession and every happiness is but lent by chance for an uncertain time, and may therefore be demanded back the next hour.

Arthur Schopenhauer

CHANGE

We must all obey the great law of change. It is the most powerful law of nature.

Edmund Burke

Change is inevitable. In a progressive country change is constant.

Benjamin Disraeli

Change is not made without inconveniences, even from worse to better.

Richard Hooker

The anticipation of change is often more upsetting than change itself, and a bit more candor would make the future a little less frightening.

Robert J. Samuelson

Change means movement, movement means friction, friction means heat, and heat means controversy. The only place where there is no friction is in outer space or a seminar on political action.

Saul Alinsky

All is flux, nothing stays still.

Heraclitus

You can build a throne out of bayonets, but you can't sit on them long.

Boris Yeltsin

During this time we have seen history made. It is as if a political ice age had ended.

Javier Perez de Cuellar

CIVILIZATION

You can't say that civilization don't advance for in every war they kill you in a new way.

Will Rogers

Civilization is the lamb's skin in which barbarianism masquerades.

Thomas B. Aldrich

Civilization advances by extending the number of important operations which we can perform without thinking about them.

Alfred North Whitehead

A nation's advance to civilization can be gauged by its treatment of the poor.

Thomas Jefferson

We are born princes and the civilizing process makes us frogs.

Eric Berne

COMMITMENT

In case of dissension, never dare to judge till you've heard the other side.

Euripides

If a man hasn't discovered something he will die for, he isn't fit to live.

Martin Luther King, Jr.

Once you pledge, don't hedge.

Nikita Khrushchev

A fellow that doesn't have any tears doesn't have any heart.

Hubert Humphrey

COMMITTEES

Outside of traffic, there is nothing that has held this country back as much as committees.

Will Rogers

When it comes to facing up to serious problems, each candidate will pledge to appoint a committee. And what is a committee? A group of the unwilling, picked from the unfit, to do the unnecessary. But it all sounds great in a campaign speech.

Richard Long Harkness

THE WIT AND WISDOM OF POLITICS

Committee—a group of men who individually can do nothing but as a group decide nothing can be done.

Fred Allen

A committee is a group that keeps the minutes and loses hours.

Milton Berle

A committee is a thing which takes a week to do what one good man can do in an hour.

Elbert Hubbard

Nothing is ever accomplished by a committee unless it consists of three members, one of whom happens to be sick and the other absent.

Hendrik van Loon

If you want to kill any idea in the world today, get a committee working on it.

Charles F. Kettering

To kill time, a committee meeting is the perfect weapon.

Laurence J. Peter

No grand idea was ever born in a conference, but a lot of foolish ideas have died there.

F. Scott Fitzgerald

A cul-de-sac to which ideas are lured and then quietly strangled.

Sir Barnett Cocks

If Moses had been a committee, the Israelites would still be in Egypt.

J.B. Hughes

If a committee is allowed to discuss a bad idea long enough, it will inevitably vote to implement the idea simply because so much work has already been done on it.

Ken Cruickshank

All committee reports conclude that, "It is not prudent to change the policy (or procedure, or organization, or whatever) at this time."

Thomas L. Martin, Jr.

I hate being placed on committees. They are always having meetings at which half are absent and the rest late.

Oliver Wendell Holmes, Jr.

CHUCK HENNING

I find it very useful to be a member of plenty of committees; I can point to the list whenever I am asked to do anything which might involve real work, and ask how I can be expected to shoulder any new duties.
Robertson Davies

Committees are to get everybody together and homogenize their thinking.
Art Linkletter

We always carry out by committee anything in which any one of us alone would be too reasonable to persist.
Frank Moore Colby

Meetings are indispensable when you don't want to do something.
John K. Galbraith

People in groups tend to agree on courses of action which, as individuals, they know are stupid.
The Abilene Paradox

Camel—a horse that was designed by a committee.
Proverb

No committee could ever come up with anything as revolutionary as a camel—anything as practical and as perfectly designed to perform effectively under such difficult conditions.
Laurence J. Peter

The person who misses the meeting is generally assigned to the work committee.
Charles Conrad III

The length of a meeting rises with the square of the number of people present.
Eileen Shanahan

I said what is very true, that any committee is only as good as the most knowledgeable, determined, and vigorous person on it. There must be somebody who provides the flame.
Lady Bird Johnson

Dochter's Dictum. Somewhere, right now, there's a committee deciding your future; only you weren't invited.
The Official Explanations

Search all the parks
In all of your cities . . .
You'll find no monuments
To any committees.

Anonymous

We made no progress at all . . . and we didn't intend to. That's the function of a national committee.

Ronald Reagan

COMMON SENSE

But no, that would be common sense—and out of place in a government.
Mark Twain

Nothing astonishes man so much as common sense and plain dealing.
Ralph Waldo Emerson

A man of great common sense and good taste,—meaning thereby a man without originality or moral courage.

George Bernard Shaw

Common sense is in spite of, not the result of, education.
Victor Hugo

Just because it's common sense, doesn't mean it's common practice.
Will Rogers

COMMUNICATION

Creative semantics is the key to contemporary government: it consists of talking in strange tongues lest the public learn the inevitable inconveniently early.

George Will

A politician must often talk and act before he has thought and read. He may be very ill-informed respecting a question; all his notions about it may be vague and inaccurate; but speak he must; and if he is a man of talents, of tact, and of intrepidity, he soon finds that, even under such circumstances, it is possible to speak successfully.

Thomas B. Macaulay

The necessity of saying something, the embarrassment produced by the consciousness of having nothing to say, and the desire to exhibit ability, are three things sufficient to render even a great man ridiculous.

Voltaire

People will accept your idea much more readily if you tell them Benjamin Franklin said it first.

David H. Comins

Don't write so that you can be understood . . . write so you can't be misunderstood.

William H. Taft (attr.)

Some things have got to be stated obscurely before they can be stated clearly.

Oliver Wendell Holmes

Former Senate Majority Leader Howard Baker of Tennessee tells a story about the time he completed his first trial. He turned to his father, also an attorney, and asked: "How'd I do father?" His father replied:

Son, you've got to guard against speaking more clearly than you think.

Sometimes people mistake the way I talk for what I am thinking.

Idi Amin

The right to speak is of little value if no one is listening.

Robert Cirino

The reason why we have two ears and only one mouth is that we may listen the more and talk the less.

Zeno of Citium

It would be interesting to analyze how many false declarations, how many fatal misunderstandings, have arisen from such pleasant qualities as shyness, consideration, affability, or ordinary good manners.

Sir Harold Nicolson

Use short, terse words. Don't perpetuate polysyllabic obfuscation.

Anonymous

COMPROMISE

I learned one thing in politics. If you go into it . . . then sooner or later you'll have to compromise. You either compromise or get out.

Hugh Sloan

If you can find something everyone agrees on, it's wrong.

Morris Udall

THE WIT AND WISDOM OF POLITICS

Compromise used to mean that half a loaf was better than no bread. Among modern statesmen it really seems to mean that half a loaf is better than a whole loaf.

G.K. Chesterton

The art of dividing a cake in such a way that everyone believes he has the biggest piece.

Ludwig Erhard

Compromise makes a good umbrella, but a poor roof; it is a temporary expedient, often wise in party politics, almost sure to be unwise in statesmanship.

James Russell Lowell

Compromise? Of course we compromise. But compromise, if not the spice of life, is its solidity. It is what makes nations great and marriages happy. . . .

Phyllis McGinley

If you cannot catch a bird of paradise, better take a wet hen.

Nikita Khrushchev

It is compromise that prevents each set of reformers . . . from crushing the group on the extreme opposite end of the political spectrum.

John F. Kennedy

All government, indeed every human benefit and enjoyment, every virtue, and every prudent act, is founded on compromise and barter. We balance inconveniences; we give and take—we remit some rights that we may enjoy others. . . .

Edmund Burke

All legislation, all government, all society is founded upon the principle of mutual concession, politeness, comity, courtesy; upon these everything is based. . . . Let him who elevates himself above humanity, above its weaknesses, its infirmities, its wants, its necessities, say, if he pleases, I will never compromise; but let no one who is not above the frailties of our common nature disdain compromises.

Henry Clay

You don't compromise principles, but you harmonize tactics to preserve unity.

John McCormick

A lean compromise is better than a fat lawsuit.

George Herbert

Reformers who are always compromising have not yet grasped the idea that truth is the only safe ground to stand on.
Elizabeth Cady Stanton

When one has been threatened with a great injustice, one accepts a smaller as a favour.
Jane Welsh Carlyle

An ignoble truce between the duty of a man and the terror of a coward.
Reginald Wright Kauffman

Don't compromise yourself. You are all you've got.
Janis Joplin

You need not fear that I shall vote for any compromise or do anything inconsistent with the past.
Daniel Webster

From the beginning of our history the country has been afflicted with compromise. It is by compromise that human rights have been abandoned.
Charles Sumner

The cause for which the battle is waged is compromised within lines clearly and distinctly defined. It should never be compromised. It is the people's cause.
Grover Cleveland

It is a weak man who urges compromise—never the strong man.
Elbert Hubbard

Compromise is but the sacrifice of one right or good in the hope of retaining another—too often ending in the loss of both.
Tyron Edwards

Those who are inclined to compromise never make a revolution.
Kemal Atatürk

If Compromise continues, the Revolution disappears.
V.I. Lenin

A revolution does not march a straight line. It wanders where it can, retreats before superior forces, advances wherever it has room, attacks whenever the enemy retreats or bluffs and, above all, is possessed of enormous patience.
Mao Tse-tung

We must be willing to learn the lesson that cooperation may imply compromise, but if it brings a world advance it is a gain for each individual nation.

Anna Eleanor Roosevelt

Most people hew the battlements of life from compromise, erecting their impregnable keeps from judicious submissions, fabricating their philosophical drawbridges from emotional reactions and scalding marauders in the boiling oil of sour grapes.

Zelda Fitzgerald

We are of course a nation of differences. These differences don't make us weak. They're the source of our strength.

James Earl Carter, Jr.

I'm a fellow who works in the vineyard of compromise.

Dan Rostenkowski

[A consensus] . . . means "everyone agrees to say collectively what no one believes individually."

Abba Eban

CONGRESS

I have been a member of the House of Representatives . . . twenty years. During the whole of that time we have been attacked, denounced, despised, hunted, harried, blamed, looked down upon, excoriated, and flayed. I refuse to take it personally. I have looked into history. I find that we did not start being unpopular when I became a Congressman. We were unpopular when Lincoln was a Congressman. We were unpopular even when Henry Clay was a Congressman. We have always been unpopular. From the beginning of the Republic it has been the duty of every free-born voter to look down upon us, and the duty of every free-born humorist to make jokes at us.

Nicholas Longworth

It is said that the titles of most bills in Congress are like the titles of Marx Brothers movies (*Duck Soup, Animal Crackers*): they do not tell much about the contents.

George Will

A House debate, encountered after its start and left before its finish, might as well be conducted in Lithuanian for all the clarity it offers.

Roderick MacLeish

The House of Representatives: A large body of egos surrounded on all four sides by lobbyists.

Anonymous

A Congressman ought to be limited to one term . . . make him come home and live under the laws he helped pass.

Anonymous

Congress is so strange. A man gets up to speak and says nothing. Nobody listens, and then everybody disagrees.

Boris Marshalov

Einstein's theory of relativity, as practiced by Congressmen, simply means getting members of your family on the payroll.

James H. Boren

Congress—these, for the most part, illiterate hacks whose fancy vests are spotted with gravy and whose speeches, hypocritical, unctuous and slovenly, are spotted also with the gravy of political patronage.

Mary McCarthy

A lot of congressmen and senators like to draw their breath and their salaries and not do much else.

Sam Ervin

When I was in the House, I was told that the difference between the House Foreign Affairs Committee and the Senate Foreign Relations Committee was that Senators were too old to have affairs. They only have relations.

Alben Barkley

I do believe we spend a lot of time doing very little, and that may be an understatement.

Robert Dole

Reader, suppose you were an idiot. And suppose you were a member of Congress. But I repeat myself.

Mark Twain

Congress is the most interesting body I have found yet. It does more crazy things, and does them with a graver earnestness, than any State Legislature that exists, perhaps.

Mark Twain

Fleas can be taught nearly anything that a Congressman can.

Mark Twain

It is the will of God that we have Congressmen, and we must bear the burden.

Mark Twain

It could probably be shown by facts and figures that there is no distinctly native American criminal class except Congress.

Mark Twain

At times the whole Senate seemed to catch hysterics of nervous bucking without apparent reason.

Henry Adams

A congressman is a pig. The only way to get his snout from the trough is to rap it sharply with a stick.

Henry Adams

I have reached the conclusion that one useless man is called a disgrace; that two are called a law firm; and that three or more become a Congress.

John Adams

People ask me where I get my jokes. Why, I just watch Congress and report the facts; I don't even have to exaggerate.

Will Rogers

The country has come to feel the same when Congress is in session as when the baby gets hold of a hammer.

Will Rogers

You know [Congressmen] are the nicest fellows in the world to meet. I sometimes really wonder if they realize the harm they do.

Will Rogers

The trouble with Senators is the ones that ought to get out don't.

Will Rogers

The bad part about our whole structure of paying our congressmen is that we name a sum and give 'em all the same, regardless of ability. No other business in the world has a fixed sum to pay all their employees the same salary. If some efficiency expert would work out a scheme where each one would be paid according to his ability, we would save a lot of money.

Will Rogers

A Congressman is never any better than his roads, and sometimes worse.

Will Rogers

CHUCK HENNING

Professor Woodrow Wilson—later to become President Wilson—described the House in the 1880s as follows:

A disintegrate mass of jarring elements.

Thomas Jefferson once expressed this keen observation about the House:

... That 150 lawyers should do business together is not to be expected.

We generally lounge or squabble the greater part of the session and crowd into a few days of the last term three or four times the business done during as many preceding months. You may therefore guess at the deliberations of Congress, when you can't hear, for the soul of you, what's going on, nor no one knows what it is, but three or four, and when it's no use to try to know.

Davy Crockett

I believe if we introduced the Lord's Prayer here . . . Senators would propose a large number of amendments to it.

Henry Wilson

The boys are in such a mood that if someone introduced the Ten Commandments they'd cut 'em down to eight.

Norris Cotton

[The Senate] . . . a legislative chamber of imposing power which sometimes finds it impossible to act; an institution heavy with tradition whose members occasionally act like school boys on a spree; a group of men with far more than their share of wisdom who sometimes act like knaves and fools; an organization with an unequaled opportunity to educate and lead the people which, at times, has served as an awesome engine of oppression.

Donald Matthews

We have the same percentage of light weights in Congress as you have in your home town. After all, it's representative government.

Alan Simpson

He who appoints those committees is an autocrat of the first magnitude.

Woodrow Wilson

The career of a member of [the] House . . . is determined, except in rare cases, by his assignment to committees.

George Hoar

The truth is, however, that a man regardless of ability must be blessed with a good prostate and liver to last it out long enough to accede to a top chairmanship. With the wisdom of a Disraeli and legislative acumen of a Tom Watson the same man would never make it without highly durable inner equipment, for the chase is unbelievably long. To the elderly goes the chairmanship; to the rheumy-eyed and palsied, credit for vision and vigor.

Merriman Smith

We see our own budgets going up for staff. There's more staff here than we need. They're all nice people. But the more staff you have, the more ideas you have, and most of them cost money. I haven't had many staff people come in with ideas to save money. It's always some new program to get their boss out front.

Robert Dole

All of us in the Senate live in an iron lung—the iron lung of politics—and it is no easy task to emerge from that rarified atmosphere in order to breathe the same fresh air our constituents breathe.

John F. Kennedy

They don't know what a grass roots movement is. They think a grass roots movement is a consensus among their staff.

Norman D'Amours

I think the people always give a sigh of relief whenever Congress goes home. I do not suppose it is all that bad, but there comes a time when the members need to go home. They need to refresh themselves and, like Antaeus, increase their strength tenfold by touching the earth of their home constituencies.

Hugh Scott

Being an Administrative Assistant to a Congressman is kind of like being married to Elizabeth Taylor. You've had some interesting experiences, but you're not sure you'd want to go through the whole thing again.

Larry King

I was never worried about any sex investigation in Washington. All the men on my staff can type.

Bella Abzug

A safe district maketh a man courageous.

Diane Rees

The best system is to have one party govern and the other party watch.

Thomas B. Reed

All the wisdom in the world consists in shouting with the majority.
Thomas B. Reed

The House has more sense than anyone in it.
Thomas B. Reed

They never open their mouths without subtracting from the sum of human knowledge.
Thomas B. Reed
on two members of the House

A thing of beauty and a jaw forever.
Thomas B. Reed
on J. Hamilton Lewis

The reputation of the Congress is lower than quail crap.
Alan Simpson

They [constituents] are always very relieved when Congress is not in session.
David H. Pryor

CONSERVATIVES

A man who believes nothing should be done for the first time.
Albert E. Wiggam

One who will not look at the new moon, out of respect for that ancient institution, the old one.
Douglas Jerrold

A man who believes in reform, but not now.
Mort Sahl

A man who wears both a belt and suspenders.
Old definition

What is conservatism? Is it not adherence to the old and tried, against the new and untried?
Abraham Lincoln

One who is against the Democrats for what they are and against the Republicans for what they are not.
Anonymous

A man who just sits and thinks, mostly sits.
Woodrow Wilson

There is always a certain meanness in the argument of conservatism, joined with a certain superiority in its fact.

Ralph Waldo Emerson

Men are conservatives when they are least vigorous, or when they are most luxurious. They are conservatives after dinner.

Ralph Waldo Emerson

A conservative is a man who is too cowardly to fight and too fat to run.

Elbert Hubbard

When a nation's young men are conservative, its funeral bell is already rung.

Henry Ward Beecher

A conservative is a person who was a liberal when young and has not changed his mind.

Samuel Beer

A Conservative is a fellow who is standing athwart history yelling "Stop."

William F. Buckley, Jr.

Conservatism is the worship of dead revolutions.

Clinton Rossiter

Conservatism offers no redress for the present, and makes no preparation for the future.

Benjamin Disraeli

It seems to be a barren thing this Conservatism—an unhappy cross-breed, the mule of politics that engenders nothing.

Benjamin Disraeli

The principle of Conservatism has always appeared to me to be not only foolish, but to be actually felo-de-se: it destroys what it loves, because it will not mend it.

Thomas Arnold

The Conservatives should never disregard political and social reform, but if there is any lesson to be learnt from history, I believe it is that the party cannot expect to win success by outbidding the radicals. This merely muddles the Conservative Party's traditional supporters and it does not actually capture the radical vote.

Lord Robert Blake

Come, come my conservative friend, wipe the dew off your spectacles and see that the world is moving.

Elizabeth Cady Stanton

I shall not grow conservative with age.

Elizabeth Cady Stanton

It's symptomatic of conservatives to say someone isn't conservative enough and isn't in tune with conservatives.

John R. Kasich

CONSERVATIVES/LIBERALS

A conservative is a statesman who is enamored of existing evils, as distinguished from the liberal who wishes to replace them with others.

Ambrose Bierce

The radical of one century is the conservative of the next. The radical invents the views. When he has worn them out the conservative adopts them.

Mark Twain

Conservatism goes for comfort, reform for truth.

Ralph Waldo Emerson

Conservatism makes no poetry, breathes no prayer, has no invention; it is all memory. Reform has no gratitude, no prudence, no husbandry.

Ralph Waldo Emerson

The conservative who resists change is as valuable as the radical who proposes it.

Will and Ariel Durant

A conservative is a man with two perfectly good legs who, however, has never learned to walk forwards ... a reactionary is a somnambulist walking backwards ... a radical is a man with both feet firmly planted— in the air.

Franklin D. Roosevelt

A conservative sees a man drowning fifty feet from shore, throws him twenty-five feet of rope, and tells him to start swimming. A liberal will throw him fifty feet of rope, then drop his end, saying he has to go off to do another good deed.

Anonymous

Liberalism is trust of the people tempered by prudence; conservatism, distrust of the people tempered by fear.

William Gladstone

So we may put him [John Dalton] down as a liberal-conservative, which perhaps may be defined as a man who thinks things ought to progress, but would rather they remained as they are.

Sir James Fitzjames Stephen

I think I am guilty of no absurdity in calling myself an advanced conservative liberal.

Anthony Trollope

The healthy stomach is nothing if not conservative. Few radicals have good digestions.

Samuel Butler (novelist)

I am not even sure what it means when one says that he is a conservative in fiscal affairs and a liberal in human affairs. I assume what it means is that you will strongly recommend the building of a great many schools to accommodate the needs of our children, but not provide the money.

Adlai Stevenson

Moderate progressivism: Don't just do something—stand there.

Adlai Stevenson

CONSISTENCY

If a politician murders his mother, the first response of the press or of his opponents will likely be not that it was a terrible thing to do, but rather that in a statement made six years before he had gone on record as being opposed to matricide.

Meg Greenfield

Nothing that isn't a real crime makes a man appear so contemptible and little in the eyes of the world as inconsistency.

Joseph Addison

Persistence in one opinion has never been considered a merit in political leaders.

Cicero

Stubborn and ardent clinging to one's opinion is the best proof of stupidity.

Michel de Montaigne

CHUCK HENNING

There is nothing in this world constant, but inconsistency.

Jonathan Swift

Consistency is the last refuge of the unimaginative.

Oscar Wilde

The only completely consistent people are the dead.

Aldous Huxley

Like all weak men he laid an exaggerated stress on not changing one's mind.

W. Somerset Maugham

A foolish consistency is the hobgoblin of little minds, adored by little statesmen and philosophers and divines. With consistency a great soul has simply nothing to do. He may as well concern himself with his shadow on the wall. Speak what you think now in hard words, and tomorrow speak what tomorrow thinks in hard words again, though it contradict everything you said today.

Ralph Waldo Emerson

I wish to say what I think and feel today, with the proviso that tomorrow perhaps I shall contradict it all.

Ralph Waldo Emerson

Inconsistencies of opinion, arising from changes of circumstances, are often justifiable.

Daniel Webster

Consistency requires you to be as ignorant today as you were a year ago.

Bernard Berenson

The only man who can change his mind is a man that's got one.

Edward Noyes Westcott

Don't be "consistent," but be simply true.

Oliver Wendell Holmes

If you have always done it that way, it is probably wrong.

Charles F. Kettering

The *Emporia Gazette* is the best loved paper in Kansas because its editor never looks into yesterday's files to see if what he proposes to write today is consistent.

Willliam Allen White

Consistency is a paste jewel that only cheap men cherish.
William Allen White

When a man you like switches from what he said a year ago, or four years ago, he is a broadminded person who has courage enough to change his mind with changing conditions. When a man you don't like does it, he is a liar who has broken his promises.
Franklin P. Adams

I have my faults, but changing my tune is not one of them.
Samuel Beckett

CONSTITUTION

Some men look at constitutions with sanctimonious reverence, and deem them like the ark of the covenant, too sacred to be touched.
Thomas Jefferson

At the other extreme is the story about New York Congressman "Tim" Campbell—one of the Tammany crowd—who once asked President Grover Cleveland to sign a pension bill that Cleveland felt was unconstitutional. Campbell is reported to have draped his arm around the President's shoulder and asked:

What's the Constitution between friends?

Whenever the Constitution comes between men and the virtue of the white women of South Carolina, I say—to hell with the Constitution.
Cole Blease

The American Constitution is the most wonderful work ever struck off at a given time by the brain and purpose of man.
William Gladstone

Your Constitution is all sail and no anchor.
Thomas B. Macaulay

I have never been more struck by the good sense and practical judgment of the Americans than in the manner in which they elude the numberless difficulties resulting from their Federal Constitution.
Alexis de Tocqueville

It is, Sir, the people's Constitution, the people's government, made for the people, made by the people, and answerable to the people.
Daniel Webster

I agree to this Constitution with all its faults, if they are such; because I think a general Government necessary for us, and there is no form of Government but what may be a blessing to the people if well administered, and believe farther that this is likely to be well administered for a course of years. . . . I doubt too whether any other convention we can obtain may be able to make a better Constitution. For when you assemble a number of men to have the advantage of their joint wisdom, you inevitably assemble with those men, all their prejudices, their passions, their errors of opinion, their local interests, and their selfish views. From such an assembly can a perfect production be expected? It therefore astonishes me, Sir, to find this system approaching so near to perfection as it does; and I think it will astonish our enemies. . . . Thus I consent, Sir, to this Constitution because I expect no better, and because I am not sure, that it is not the best. The opinions I have had of its errors, I sacrifice to the public good.

Benjamin Franklin

Our Constitution is in actual operation; everything appears to promise that it will last; but in this world nothing can be said to be certain, except death and taxes.

Benjamin Franklin

We are under a Constitution, but the Constitution is what the judges say it is.

Charles Evans Hughes

In essence, the Constitution is not a literary composition but a way of ordering society, adequate for imaginative statesmanship, if judges have imagination for statesmanship.

Felix Frankfurter

Constitutions are checks upon the hasty action of the majority. They are the self-imposed restraints of a whole people upon a majority of them to secure sober action and a respect for the rights of the minority.

William H. Taft

Everybody talks of the constitution, but all sides forget that the constitution is extremely well, and would do very well, if they would but let it alone.

Horace Walpole

"We, the people." It is a very eloquent beginning, but when that document was completed on the seventeenth of September in 1787 I was not included in the "We, the people." I felt somehow for many years that George Washington and Alexander Hamilton just left me out by mistake. But through the process of amendment, interpretation and court decision I have finally been included in "We, the people."

Barbara Jordan

There is nothing new in the realization that the Constitution sometimes insulates the criminality of a few in order to protect the privacy of us all.

Antonin Scalia

CONSULTANTS

Well, we won that election 54 to 46 percent. I didn't do it all, but hell, I have to take the blame when we lose, so I guess I can claim credit if we win.

Matt Reese

A consultant is a man who knows fifty different ways to make love, but doesn't know any women.

Anonymous

Consultant: one who looks at your watch and tells you what time it is.

Anonymous

For a mere half-million dollars, he'll advise you not to drool on national television.

Ann Richards

CONTRIBUTIONS

Money is the mother's milk of politics.

Jesse Unruh

There are two things that are important in politics. The first is money, and I can't remember what the second one is.

Mark Hanna

Money to a politician is like legs to a hockey player. When they go, you're finished.

Bob Perkins

It costs a fortune in politics to get beat.

Finley Peter Dunne

When there is money in an election, it's always in doubt.

Will Rogers

Take your campaign contribution, and send it to the Red Cross, and let the election be decided on its merit.

Will Rogers

I just received the following wire from my generous Daddy—"Dear Jack—Don't buy a single vote more than necessary . . . I'll be damned if I'm going to pay for a landslide."

John F. Kennedy

On this matter of experience, I had announced earlier this year that if successful I would not consider campaign contributions as a substitute for experience in appointing ambassadors. Ever since I made that statement I have not received one single cent from my father.

John F. Kennedy

With the money I'm spending I could elect my chauffeur.

Joseph P. Kennedy

If you can't raise money in your own state you're in trouble.

Lyndon B. Johnson

The civil service gang is always howlin' about candidates and office-holders puttin' up money for campaigns and about corporations chippin' in. They might as well howl about givin' contributions to churches. A political organization has to have money for its business as well as a church, and who has more right to put up than the men who get the good things that are goin'.

George Washington Plunkitt

If you want to be part of this system, you've got to put your money where your mouth is.

Edward Forgotson

The food at political fund-raisers should be just good enough so people don't complain too long.

Bradley S. O'Leary

Contribution: Slush fund.
Slush fund: Contribution (the difference being whether you're talking about yours or theirs).

Merriman Smith

Some of us are uncomfortable taking honoraria. I am uncomfortable taking campaign contributions. So, I compromised; I decided to take both.

Robert Dole

Come with me now and you'll have a friend in the Senate. Come with me in two months and my door will always be open. Come with me after the election and I promise you good government.

Russell Long (attr.)

He gives twice who gives soon because he will soon be called upon to give again.

Benjamin Franklin

The Congressional campaign system has become toxic with money. We chafe over the burden of having to take our time to go, tin cup in hand, begging to PACs for the money to run for public office. Yet we have it in our power to stop the madness.

Robert C. Byrd

[To restrict political spending] ... is much like allowing a speaker in a public hall to express his views while denying him the use of an amplifying system.

William H. Rehnquist

The price of running for the Senate today is spending more time than you'd like to spend asking people for more money than they'd like to give.

Harriet Woods

CONVENTIONS

There is something about a national convention that makes it as fascinating as a revival or a hanging. It is vulgar, it is ugly, it is stupid, it is tedious, it is hard upon both the higher cerebral centers and the gluteus maximus, and yet it is somehow charming. One sits through the long sessions wishing heartily that all the delegates and alternates were dead and in hell—and suddenly there comes a show so gaudy and hilarious, so melodramatic and obscene, so unimaginably exhilarating and preposterous that one lives a gorgeous year in an hour.

H.L. Mencken

A chess tournament disguised as a circus.

Alistair Cooke

A combination iv th' Chicago fire, St. Bartholomew's massacre, the battle iv th' Boyne, the life iv Jesse James, and th' night iv th' big wind.

Finley Peter Dunne

... More wasted energy, more futile fruitless endeavor, more useless expenditure of noise, money, and talent than any institution on earth.

Irvin S. Cobb

In several ways the convention is a peculiar institution. Like an impatient Brigadoon it comes to life every four years; it is master of its own rules, and its decisions are as irrevocable as a haircut. Yet, the convention isn't even mentioned in the Constitution or in any law passed by Congress. In this sense, it might be described as the most unofficial official (or most official unofficial) gathering in politics.

David Brinkley

The dirty work at political conventions is almost always done in the grim hours between midnight and dawn. Hangmen and politicians work best when the human spirit is at its lowest ebb.

Russell Baker

A political convention is just not a place where you come away with any trace of faith in human nature.

Murray Kempton

The convention system has its faults, of course, but I do not know of a better method for choosing a presidential nominee.

Harry S. Truman

The convention is the voice, the bone and sinews of a political party— and sometimes it even nominates an Abraham Lincoln.

Fletcher Knebel

It's the one place where our public men can do foolish things and due to the surroundings they kinder look plausible at the time.

Will Rogers

I hate to say it, but the women that spoke were all terrible. Well, they were pretty near as bad as the men, that will give you an idea of how bad they were.

Will Rogers

The chairman of a state delegation is a man that announces how many votes his state casts. The qualification for his job seems to call for a man who can't count. After he has announced the votes, they poll the delegates and he sees for himself just how near he guessed.

Will Rogers

Now a delegate . . . is bad enough, but an alternate is just a spare tire for a delegate. An alternate is the lowest form of political life there is. He is the parachute on a plane that never leaves the ground.

Will Rogers

A Democratic convention has to smell the blood of a death struggle before it can decide whom it will honor.

William Allen White

A convention feels about demonstrations somewhat like the big man who had a small wife who was in the habit of beating him. When asked why he permitted it, he replied that it seemed to please her and did not hurt him.

William Jennings Bryan

Gentlemen, this is the convention of free speech, and I have been given the floor. I have only a few words to say to you, but I shall say them if I stand here until tomorrow morning.

George William Curtis

It's like a nine-day plane crash.

Mary Deibel

A man of tastes, arrived from Mars, would take one look at a convention floor and leave forever, convinced he had seen one of the drearier squats of Hell . . . a cigar-smoking, stale-aired, slack-jawed, butt-littered, foul, bleak, hard-working, bureaucratic death gas of language and faces . . . lawyers, judges, ward heelers, mafiosos, Southern goons and grandees, grande old ladies, trade unionists and finks; of pompous words and long pauses which are like a leaden pain over fever.

Norman Mailer

CORRUPTION

Vast power and wealth . . . breed commercial and political corruption and incite public favorites to dangerous ambitions.

Mark Twain

. . . In politics a certain amount of corruption is inevitable and inescapable. Purity in politics is an impractical dream.

Frank R. Kent

. . . The great mass of voters have no inherent or instinctive objection to corruption; that at heart, however they may have felt in former decades, they do not now expect or demand rigid honesty in public officials, party leaders or party candidates.

Frank R. Kent

Political corruption is not a matter of men or classes or education or character of any sort; it is a matter of pressure. Wherever the pressure is brought to bear, society and government cave in. The problem, then, is one of dealing with the pressure, of discovering and dealing with the cause or the sources of the pressure to buy and corrupt.

Lincoln Steffens

In a more modern vein, here's how U.S. Attorney Rudolph Giuliani described a 1987 FBI "sting" operation to uncover government corruption in New York State:

On 106 occasions, bribes were offered or discussed. On 105 of those occasions, the public official involved accepted the bribe. And on the other occasion, he turned it down because he didn't think the amount was large enough.

You know that if I had ever been corrupted, I wouldn't still be around.
Richard Daley

If you want to steal, steal a little cleverly, in a nice way. Only if you steal so much as to become rich overnight, you will be caught.
Mobutu Sese Seko

CRITICISM/CRITICS

Critics are like eunuchs in a harem: they know how it's done, they've seen it done every day, but they're unable to do it themselves.
Brendan Behan

I have never found in a long experience of politics, that criticism is ever inhibited by ignorance.
Harold Macmillan

I never read a book before reviewing it, it prejudices a man so.
Sydney Smith

Honest criticism is hard to take, particularly from a relative, a friend, an acquaintance, or a stranger.
Franklin P. Jones

Persecution is the first law of society because it is always easier to suppress criticism than to meet it.
Howard Mumford Jones

To criticize one's country is to do it a service and pay it a compliment. It is a service because it may spur the country to do better than it is doing; it is a compliment because it evidences a belief that a country can do better than it is doing . . . Criticism, in short is . . . an act of patriotism, a higher form of patriotism, I believe, than the familiar rituals of national adulation.
J. William Fulbright

I do not resent criticism, even when, for the sake of emphasis, it parts for the time with reality.

Winston S. Churchill

They have vilified me, they have crucified me, yes, they have even criticized me.

Richard Daley

I resent the insinuendos.

Richard Daley

DEBATES

The American custom is when you can't beat a man at anything, why the last straw is to debate him.

Will Rogers

I am bound to furnish my antagonists with arguments, but not with comprehension.

Benjamin Disraeli

Don't argue about the difficulties. The difficulties will argue for themselves.

Winston S. Churchill

When debate becomes the rule and speech-making the exception, we shall have a better state of things in that regard; for speech-making contributes more than anything else to the ruin of debate. . . . Still there are times when business propositions being numerous and the days few, one wishes that eloquence and speaking bore closer resemblance to reasoning and deliberation.

Thomas B. Reed

Our debates have been like the mating of pandas in the zoo—the expectations are high, there's a lot of fuss and commotion, but there's never any kind of result.

Bruce Babbitt

DEBT

A national debt, if it is not excessive, will be to us a national blessing.

Alexander Hamilton

I go on the principle that a Public Debt is a Public curse.
James Madison

Blessed are the young, for they shall inherit the national debt.
Herbert Hoover

The principle of spending money to be paid by posterity under the name of funding, is but swindling futurity on a large scale.
Thomas Jefferson

Borrowers are nearly always ill-spenders, and it is with lent money that all evil is mainly done, and all unjust war is protracted.
John Ruskin

We can only pay our debt to the past by putting the future in debt to ourselves.
John Buchan (Lord Tweedsmuir)

Speak not of my debts unless you mean to pay them.
Edward Herbert

As individuals, many of our senators and representatives are thoughtful and responsible public servants. As a collective body, confronted by a myriad of special interest groups, however, Congress has the backbone of a freshly boiled noodle and the firmness of an overripe avocado without the pit. Senior administration officials who three years ago would have been horrified by a $180 billion deficit in the second year of a recovery now seem to view this misbegotten child of some of their own policies as at least socially acceptable, if not downright beautiful.
Michael Mussa

Christmas is a time when kids tell Santa what they want and adults pay for it. Deficits are when adults tell the government what they want—and their kids pay for it.
Richard Lamm

DEFENSE
He who defends everything defends nothing.
Frederick the Great

"Thrice is he armed that hath his quarrel just"—And four times he who gets his fist in fust.
Artemus Ward

Am I wrong in listening to women who live in Nicaragua and follow the Sermon on the Mount? Or am I supposed to sit here and believe generals?

Thomas P. O'Neill

Fear is no basis for foreign policy.

Margaret Thatcher

All wars are wars among thieves who are too cowardly to fight and who therefore induce the young manhood of the whole world to do their fighting for them.

Emma Goldman

We are going to have peace, even if we have to fight for it.

Dwight David Eisenhower

DEMAGOGUES

A man who can rock the boat himself and persuade everybody there's a terrible storm at sea.

Anonymous

A demagogue is a person with whom we disagree as to which gang should mismanage the country.

Don Marquis

The demagogue is one who preaches doctrines he knows to be untrue to men he knows to be idiots.

H.L. Mencken

The demagogue, whether of the Right or Left, is consciously or unconsciously, an undetected liar.

Walter Lippmann

In every age the vilest specimens of human nature are to be found among demagogues.

Thomas B. Macaulay

The peculiar office of a demagogue is to advance his own interests, by affecting a deep devotion to the interests of the people. Sometimes the object is to indulge malignancy, unprincipled and selfish men submitting but to two governing motives, that of doing good to themselves, and that of harm to others. The true theater of a demagogue is a democracy, for the body of the community possessing the power, the master he pretends to serve is best able to award his efforts.

James Fenimore Cooper

The sure foundations of the state are laid in knowledge, not in ignorance. Every sneer at education, at culture, at book learning—which is the recorded wisdom of the experiences of mankind—is the demagogue's sneer at intelligent liberty, inviting national degeneracy and ruin.

George William Curtis

History teaches that among the men who have overturned the liberties of republics, the greatest number have begun their career by paying an obsequious court to the people; commencing demagogues, and ending tyrants.

Alexander Hamilton

DEMOCRACY

Many forms of government have been tried, and will be tried in this world of sin and woe. No one pretends that democracy is perfect or all-wise. Indeed, it has been said that democracy is the worst form of government except all those other forms that have been tried from time to time.

Winston S. Churchill

Democracy is good. I say this because other systems are worse.

Jawaharlal Nehru

Monarchy is like a splendid ship, with all sails set; it moves majestically on, then it hits a rock and sinks forever. Democracy is like a raft. It never sinks, but, damn it, your feet are always in the water.

Fisher Ames

Democracy is a device that insures we shall be governed no better than we deserve.

George Bernard Shaw

Democracy substitutes election by the incompetent many for appointment by the corrupt few.

George Bernard Shaw

I do not believe in democracy but am willing to admit it provides the only amusing form of government ever endured by mankind.

H.L. Mencken

Democracy is the art and science of running the circus from the monkey cage.

H.L. Mencken

On account of us being a democracy and run by the people, we are the only nation in the world that has to keep a government four years, no matter what it does.

Will Rogers

The Greeks

Our constitution is named a democracy, because it is in the hands not of the few but of the many.

Thucydides

Democracy . . . is a charming form of government, full of variety and disorder, and dispensing a sort of equality to equals and unequals alike.

Plato

A democracy is a government in the hands of men of low birth, no property, and unskilled labor.

Aristotle

The basis of a democratic state is liberty.

Aristotle

The French

Were there a people of gods, their government would be democratic.

Jean-Jacques Rousseau

In the strict sense of the term, a true democracy has never existed and never will.

Jean-Jacques Rousseau

Democratic nations are but little for what has been, but they are haunted by visions of what will be; in this direction their unbounded imagination grows and dilates beyond all measure.

Alexis de Tocqueville

Democracy is the name we give to the people each time we need them.

Robert de Flers

The British

An aristocracy of blackbirds.

Lord Byron

Democracy is, by the nature of it, a self-cancelling business; and gives in the long run a net result of zero.

Thomas Carlyle

Democracy means simply the bludgeoning of the people, by the people, for the people.

Oscar Wilde

The world is weary of statesmen whom democracy has degraded into politicians.

Benjamin Disraeli

Democracy means government by the uneducated, while aristocracy means government by the badly educated.

G.K. Chesterton

It is not the business of politicians, in our sort of democracy, to make other men good in their own image of goodness; it is to give them the chance of being as good as they choose.

London economist

We should be nearer the mark, and should have a far more convincing slogan if we spoke of the need, not to defend democracy, but to create it.

E.H. Carr

In England it is bad manners to be clever, to assert something confidently. It may be your personal view that two and two makes four, but you must not state it in a self-assured way because this is a democratic country and others may be of a different opinion.

George Mikes

The republican form of government is the highest type of government; but because of this it requires the highest type of human nature—a type nowhere at present existing.

Herbert Spencer

Our great democracies still seem to think that a stupid man is more likely to be honest than a clever man, and there are politicians who take advantage of this prejudice by pretending to be even more stupid than nature made them.

Bertrand Russell

Whatever may be truly said about the good sense of a democracy during a great crisis, at ordinary times it does not bring the best men to the top.

William R. Inge

Democracy means government by discussion, but it is only effective if you can stop people talking.

Clement Attlee

In a pure democracy the ruling men will be the wirepullers and their friends.

Sir James Fitzjames Stephen

Democracy is inflation.

C. Northcote Parkinson

A democracy in which everybody had an equal responsibility in everything would be oppressive for the conscientious and licentious for the rest.

T.S. Eliot

Other Countries
Democracy is the abuse of statistics.

Jorge Luis Borges

In democracy the people elect a leader in whom they have confidence. Then the elected leader says: "Now shut up and obey me." People and parties may no longer meddle in what he says.

Max Weber

The democracy which embodies and guarantees our freedom is not powerless, passive or blind, nor is it in retreat. It has no intention of giving way to the savage fantasies of its adversaries. It is not prepared to give advance blessing to its own destruction.

Pierre Elliott Trudeau

Without glasnost there is not, and there cannot be, democratism, the political creativity of the masses and their participation in management.

Mikhail Gorbachev

The Americans
Democracies have ever been spectacles of turbulence and contention.

James Madison

As I would not be a slave, so I would not be a master. This expresses my idea of democracy.

Abraham Lincoln

Democracy is based on the conviction that man has the moral and intellectual capacity, as well as the inalienable right, to govern himself with reason and justice.

Harry S. Truman

Democracy is the superior form of government because it is based on a respect for man as a reasonable being.

John F. Kennedy

Democracy, as I understand it, requires me to sacrifice myself for the masses, not to them. Who knows not that if you would save the people, you must often oppose them.

John C. Calhoun

All the ills of democracy can be cured by more democracy.

Al Smith

Democracy is liberty plus economic security. We Americans want to pray, think as we please—and eat regular.

Maury Maverick

Self-criticism is the secret weapon of democracy, and candor and confession are good for the political soul.

Adlai Stevenson

Democracy becomes a government of bullies tempered by editors.

Ralph Waldo Emerson

Democracy is that form of society, no matter what its political classification, in which every man has a chance and knows that he has it.

James Russell Lowell

It is a besetting vice of democracies to substitute public opinion for law. This is the usual form in which masses of men exhibit their tyranny.

James Fenimore Cooper

Political democracy, as it exists and practically works in America, with all its threatening evils, supplies a training school for making first-class men. It is life's gymnasium, not of good only, but of all.

Walt Whitman

Democracy never comes so close to destroying itself as when it is attempting to perpetuate itself by free elections.

Irving Stone

In a democracy the general good is furthered only when the special interests of competing minorities accidentally coincide—or cancel each other out.

Alexander Chase

In a democracy, the opposition is not only tolerated as constitutional, but must be maintained because it is indispensable.

Walter Lippmann

A democratic society might be defined as one . . . in which the majority is always prepared to put down a revolutionary minority.

Walter Lippmann

Democracy is the recurrent suspicion that more than half of the people are right more than half of the time.

E.B. White

The blind lead the blind. It's the democratic way.

Henry Miller

Democracy is based on the conviction that there are extraordinary possibilities in ordinary people.

H.E. Fosdick

Man's capacity for justice makes democracy possible, but man's inclination to injustice makes democracy necessary.

Reinhold Niebuhr

Democracy is finding proximate solutions to insoluble problems.

Reinhold Niebuhr

The greatest blessing of our democracy is freedom. But in the last analysis, our only freedom is the freedom to discipline ourselves.

Bernard Baruch

Democracy is a small hard core of common agreement, surrounded by a rich variety of individual differences.

James B. Conant

In contrast to totalitarianism, a democracy can face and live with the truth about itself.

Sidney Hook

Everybody believes in democracy until he reaches the White House.

Thomas Cronin

Democracy is that form of government where everybody gets what the majority deserves.

James Dale Davidson

In free countries, every man is entitled to express his opinions—and every other man is entitled not to listen.

G. Norman Collie

Democracy is a process by which the people are free to choose the man who will get the blame.

Laurence J. Peter

Democracy: in which you can say what you like and do as you're told.

Gerald Barry

In a democratic society like ours, relief must come through an aroused popular conscience that sears the conscience of the people's representatives.

Felix Frankfurter

The function of our complex constitutional structure is to extract what wisdom is available in the people, at any moment in time, and give it a role in government.

Irving Kristol

Democracy is rather like sex. When it's good, it's very very good. And when it's bad, it's still pretty good.

John Akar

As citizens of this democracy you are the rulers and the ruled, the lawgivers and the law-abiding, the beginning and the end.

Adlai Stevenson

Democracy is measured not by its leaders doing extraordinary things, but by its citizens doing ordinary things extraordinarily well.

John Gardner

The disclosure mania will make for more cliques that meet privately before hand to agree on concerted actions subsequently revealed only at the public meeting.

Warren Bennis

DEMOCRATIC PARTY

We live in a world of sin and sorrow. Otherwise there would not be any Democratic Party.

Thomas B. Reed

Nobody can lead this wrangling, quarrelsome, factionalized Democratic minority.

Charles Crisp

Democrats are excitable, difficult to lead, idealistic and reckless when in convention assembled. History demonstrates that they would rather fight among themselves than with the enemy. When Republican delegations are released from their home instructions, they go to their bosses. When Democratic delegations are released, they go to pieces.

Arthur Krock

Any well-established village in New England or the northern Middle West could afford a town drunkard, a town atheist, and a few Democrats.

D.W. Brogan

The Democratic party is the party of the Poor marshalled against the Rich. . . . But they are always officered by a few self-seeking deserters from the Rich or Whig party.

Ralph Waldo Emerson

The Democratic Party is like a mule. It has neither pride of ancestry nor hope of posterity.

Ignatius Donnelly

I never said all Democrats were saloon-keepers. What I said was that all saloon-keepers were Democrats.

Horace Greeley

The Democratic party of the nation ain't dead, though it's been givin' a lifelike imitation of a corpse for several years. The trouble is that the party's been chasin' after theories and staying up nights readin' books instead of studyin' human nature and actin' accordin' . . .

George Washington Plunkitt

There is no Democratic Party and William Jennings Bryan is its leader.

Anonymous

I belong to no organized political party—I am a Democrat.

Will Rogers

There is something about a Republican that you can only stand him for just so long. And on the other hand, there is something about a Democrat that you can't stand him for quite that long.

Will Rogers

The Republicans have their splits right after the election and the Democrats have theirs just before an election.

Will Rogers

Every Harvard class should have one Democrat to rescue it from oblivion.

Will Rogers

The Democrats are the only known race of people that will give a dinner and then won't decide who will be toastmaster till they all get to the dinner and fight over it. No job is ever too small for them to split over.

Will Rogers

The young creature is a Democrat, and speaks with the native strength and inelegance of his tribe. . . . I suppose all Democrats are on sociable terms with the devil.

Mark Twain

All Democrats are insane, but not one of them knows it; none but the Republicans and Mugwumps know it. All the Republicans are insane, but only the Democrats and Mugwumps can perceive it.

Mark Twain

He . . . became so expert in duplicity . . . and so admirably plausible that he couldn't tell, himself, when he was lying and when he wasn't. Somebody told him to keep up the dodge of pretending to belong to both parties—it was first-rate Washington policy to carry water on both shoulders. George said as long as he only had to carry the water on his shoulders, he could stand it, but he was too good a Democrat to carry any in his stomach!

Mark Twain

The dimmycratic party ain't on speakin' terms with itsilf.

Finley Peter Dunne

If the Democratic Party was a woman of the Victorian era she would be at the Florence Crittendon home.

Mark Shields

The Democratic Party is not one—but two—political parties with the same name. They unite only once every two years—to wage political campaigns.

Dwight David Eisenhower

You can never underestimate the ability of the Democrats to wet their finger and hold it to the wind.

Ronald Reagan

The Democratic Party leaders are always troubadours of trouble, crooners of catastrophe. Public confusion on vital issues is Democratic weather. A Democratic President is doomed to his goals like a squid, squirting darkness about him.

Clare Boothe Luce

The Democrats are in a real bind. They won't get elected unless things get worse and things won't get worse unless they get elected.

Jeanne Kirkpatrick

A hopeless assortment of discordant differences, as incapable of positive action as it is capable of infinite clamor.

Thomas B. Reed

The Democratic Party is like a man riding backward in a railroad car; it never sees anything until it has got past it.

Thomas B. Reed

We are Republicans and don't propose to leave our party and identify ourselves with the party whose antecedents have been Rum, Romanism, and Rebellion.

S.D. Burchard

When a leader is in the Democratic Party he's a boss; when he's in the Republican Party he's a leader.

Harry S. Truman

The Democratic Party is the people's party, not the labor party, not the farmers' party, not the employees' party—it is the party of no-one because it is the party of every one. That I think is our ancient mission. Where we have deserted it, we have failed. Better we lose the election than mislead the people; better we lose than misgovern the people.

Adlai Stevenson

When the Democatic Party forms a firing squad we form a circle.

Morris Udall

The Democatic party is a mixture, an amalgam, a mosaic. Call it a fruitcake.

Jim Wright

Most of us Democrats these days are going through a kind of intellectual adolescence about what it means to have that party affiliation. It's like our policies are pimples on the face of Democratic politics. Our job is to apply an ointment on a hormonally confused party.

David Skaggs

CHUCK HENNING

**Democrats in the courtroom. The following remark is attrib-
uted to a Colorado judge who sentenced Alferd E. Packer for
cannibalism in 1874:**

There are only six Democrats in all of Hinsdale County and you, you son
of a bitch, you ate five of them.

**Comedian Mark Russell has often told of the Indiana woman
who specified in her will that she be buried just outside Chicago
so she could remain active in Democratic politics.**

Democrats are . . . the party that says government can make you richer,
smarter, taller and get the chickweed out of your lawn. Republicans are
the party that says government doesn't work, and then they get elected
to prove it.

P.J. O'Rourke

I have found that, when confronted with a problem, the automatic
reaction of high-minded, intelligent Democrats would be, "Government must do something." When Republicans of like character
confront a similar problem, the reaction is "*We* must do something."

Millicent Fenwick

DIPLOMATS

An ambassador is an honest man sent to lie abroad for the commonwealth.

Sir Henry Wotton

I have discovered the art of fooling diplomats; I speak truth and they
never believe me.

Benso di Cavour

A real diplomat is one who can cut his neighbor's throat without having
his neighbor notice it.

Trygve Lie

A diplomat is one that says something that is equally misunderstood by
both sides, and never clear to either.

Will Rogers

Diplomats are just as essential to starting a war as soldiers are for
finishing it. . . . You take diplomacy out of war, and the thing would fall
flat in a week.

Will Rogers

Diplomacy is the art of saying "nice doggie" until you can find a rock.
Anonymous

A diplomat is a man who can tell you to go to hell in such a way that you actually look forward to the trip.
Caskie Stinnett

Tact: the ability to describe others as they see themselves.
Abraham Lincoln

It is better to discuss things, to argue and engage in polemics than make perfidious plans of mutual destruction.
Mikhail Gorbachev

We have before us the opportunity to forge for ourselves and for future generations a new world order, a world where the rule of law, not the law of the jungle, governs the conduct of nations.
George Bush

DIRECTION

We're going to move left and right at the same time.
Jerry Brown

In 1952 candidate Adlai Stevenson was asked whether he was headed left, right or center. He replied:

I think it would be more relevant to ask: Is the man moving forward or backwards, or is he grounded?

We cannot move forward by running constantly to the right or to the left. Sometimes we need less government, and sometimes we need more.
Edward Kennedy

I find the great thing in this world is not so much where we stand, as in what direction we are moving. We must sail sometimes with the wind and sometimes against it—but we must sail, and not drift, nor lie at anchor.
Oliver Wendell Holmes

When you don't know where you're going any road may take you there.
Lewis Carroll

When you don't know where you're going, you'll probably end up somewhere else.
Anonymous

After all, no man goes as far as the man who does not know where he is going.

Oliver Cromwell

I suspect Cromwell was right: the man who does not know where he's going goes farthest.

Gore Vidal

One never goes so far as when one doesn't know where one is going.
Johann Wolfgang von Goethe

Then there was the lament of New Mexico Senator Pete Domenici when he was chairing the Congressional conference committee, which was struggling to reduce the federal budget deficit in July 1985:

Frankly, everywhere I turn, I don't see a way to go.

The senator could have followed the advice of the immortal one-time New York Yankees catcher Yogi Berra, who said:

When you arrive at a fork in the road—take it.

To those waiting with bated breath for that favorite media catch phrase, the U-turn, I have only one thing to say, you turn if you want to. The lady's not for turning.

Margaret Thatcher

DO-GOODERS

If I knew . . . that a man was coming to my house with the conscious design of doing me good, I should run for my life.
Henry David Thoreau

In the United States doing good has come to be, like patriotism, a favorite device of persons with something to sell.

H.L. Mencken

The urge to save humanity is almost always a false front for the urge to rule.

H.L. Mencken

Those who have given themselves the most concern about the happiness of peoples have made their neighbors very miserable.

Anatole France

Goodness without wisdom always accomplishes evil.
Robert A. Heinlein

It is not enough to do good; one must do it the right way.
John Morley

ECONOMICS/ECONOMISTS

What we might call, by way of eminence, the dismal science.
Thomas Carlyle

If our economy of freedom fails to distribute wealth as ably as it has created it, the road to dictatorship will be open to any man who can persuasively promise security to all.
Will and Ariel Durant

One of the greatest pieces of economic wisdom is to know what you do not know.
John K. Galbraith

One of the soundest rules to remember when making forecasts in the field of economics is that whatever is to happen is happening already.
Sylvia Porter

Economists have the least influence on policy where they know the most and are most agreed; they have the most influence on policy where they know the least and disagree most vehemently.
Murphy's Law of Economic Policy

When conflicting economic advice is offered, the worst will be taken.
Murphy's Corollary

What's good politics is bad economics; what's bad politics is good economics; what's good economics is bad politics; what's bad economics is good politics. Or ... what's good politics is bad economics and vice versa, vice versa.

Eugene Baer

Nine out of ten economic laws are economic laws only till they are found out.

Robert Lynd

All knowledge in the field of economics can be summed up in only nine words: There is no such thing as a free lunch.

Old adage

There are two things that can disrupt the American economy. One is a war. The other is a meeting of the Federal Reserve Board.

Will Rogers

Whenever there are great strains or changes in the economic system, it tends to generate crackpot theories, which then find their way into legislative channels.

David Stockman

In addition to these idiosyncrasies, there are general laws that influence how political decision makers react to economic conditions. One is Bert Lance's law: "If it ain't broke, don't fix it." I observe a corollary of that law, which is: "If it might break, don't go near it." This law is known as preserving deniability. A third law is: "If it does break, change something." This might be called Demosthenes' Law, because he said, "Some people think they can stump the man who mounts the tribune by asking him what is to be done. To those I will give what I believe to be the fairest and truest answer: Don't do what you are doing now."

Herbert Stein

It is not possible for this nation to be at once politically internationalist and economically isolationist. This is just as insane as asking one Siamese twin to high dive while the other plays the piano.

Adlai Stevenson

If one could divine the nature of the economic forces in the world, one could foretell the future.

Robert Heilbroner

Economic forecasting houses like Data Resources and Chase Econometrics have successfully predicted fourteen of the last five recessions.

David Fehr

The gap in our economy is between what we have and what we think we ought to have—and that is a moral problem, not an economic one.

Paul Heyne

There are in the fields of economics no constant relations, and consequently no measurement is possible. . . . Statistical figures referring to economic events are historical data. They tell us what happened in a nonrepeatable historical case.

Ludwig Edler von Mises

Economic distress will teach men, if anything can, that realities are less dangerous than fancies, that fact-finding is more effective than fault-finding.

Carl Lotus Becker

The truth seems . . . to be that in the ultimate and essential problem the economic factor is relatively superficial and unimportant.

Frank Hyneman Knight

The age of chivalry has gone. That of sophisters, economists, and calculators has succeeded, and the glory of Europe is extinguished forever.

Edmund Burke

The instability of the economy is equaled only by the instability of economists.

John H. Williams

In Canada, there is a small radical group that refuses to speak English and no one can understand them. They are Separatists. In this country we have the same kind of group. They are called Economists.

Anonymous

The one profession where you can gain great eminence without ever being right.

George Meany

Economist: A man who states the obvious in terms of the incomprehensible.

Alfred A. Knopf

An economist is someone who can look at the rumpled sheets and tell you if it was done for love or for money.

Anonymous

An economist is a man who would marry Elizabeth Taylor for her money.

Anonymous

If all the economists in the world were laid end to end, they would not reach a conclusion.

George Bernard Shaw

If all the nation's economists were laid end to end, they would point in all directions.

Arthur H. Motley

Economists now say we move in cycles instead of running around in circles. It sounds better, but it means the same.

Anonymous

Economists are almost invariably engaged in defeating the last slump.

Stuart Chase

Ask five economists and you'll get five different explanations. Six, if one went to Harvard.

Edgar A. Fiedler

Economists think the poor need them to tell them that they are poor.

Peter Drucker

In all the recorded history there has not been one economist who has had to worry about where the next meal would come from.

Peter Drucker

An economist is an expert who will know tomorrow why the things he predicted yesterday didn't happen today.

Laurence J. Peter

If economists could manage to get themselves thought of as humble, competent people, on a level with dentists, that would be splendid.

John Maynard Keynes

Practical men, who believe themselves to be quite exempt from any intellectual influences, are usually the slaves of some defunct economist. ... It is ideas, not vested interests, which are dangerous for good or evil.

John Maynard Keynes

[Economist]. Someone who's good with numbers but doesn't have the personality to be an accountant.

Anonymous

Someone who finds something in practice and wonders if it would work in theory.

Ernest Hollings

[Economists] ... can take facts and figures and bring them together, but their predictions are not worth any more than ours. If they were, they would have all the money and we would not have anything.

Bernard Baruch

I've been wrong so many times I'm beginning to sound like an economist.

Reporter on TV panel show

The good news is that a busload of supply-side economists plunged over a cliff. The bad news is that three seats were unoccupied at the time.

Morris Udall

I plan to aim for a society in which each and every Japanese person in his daily life can genuinely feel prosperous. . . . The Nation's economy is rich, but the people don't feel rich. That says something is wrong with basic Japanese policy.

Kiichi Miyazawa

The man who brought us voodoo economics has become the witch doctor of American health care. It is time to revoke the license of Doctor Bush. He is guilty of malpractice.

Robert Kerrey

EDUCATION

Intelligence appears to be the thing that enables a man to get along without education. Education appears to be the thing that enables a man to get along without the use of his intelligence.

Albert Wiggam

Education, like neurosis, begins at home.

Milton R. Saperstein

He who controls the purse strings controls the educational policy.

Furst's Academic Axiom

There is no direct relationship between the quality of an educational program and its cost.

Terman's Law

We are faced with the paradoxical fact that education has become one of the chief obstacles to intelligence and freedom of thought.

Bertrand Russell

Education produces natural intuitions, and natural intuitions are erased by education.

Pascal

Education is what you get from reading the small print. Experience is what you get from not reading it.

Saul Lavisky

The education explosion is producing a vast number of people who want to live significant, important lives but lack the ability to satisfy this craving for importance by individual achievement. The country is being swamped with nobodies who want to be somebody.

Eric Hoffer

Education is the process of moving from cocksure ignorance to thoughtful uncertainty.

Utvich's Observation

Nothing in education is as astonishing as the amount of ignorance it accumulates in the form of inert facts.

Henry Adams

The direction in which education starts a man, will determine his future life.

Plato

Education makes a people easy to lead, but difficult to drive; easy to govern but impossible to enslave.

Henry Peter Brougham

Human history more and more becomes a race between education and catastrophe.

H.G. Wells

Universities are full of knowledge; the freshmen bring a little in and the seniors take none away, and knowledge accumulates.

Abbott Lawrence Lowell

Education is the process of casting false pearls before real swine.

Irwin Edman

The avocation of assessing the failures of better men can be turned into a comfortable livelihood, providing you can back it up with a Ph. D.

Nelson Algren

I respect faith, but doubt is what gives you an education.

Wilson Mizner

Real improvement in our schools is not simply a matter of spending more, it is a matter of expecting more.

George Bush

You must not choose entertainment over education. Young America, you cannot make VCRs, being calm, cool and laid back. You must know math and science.

Jesse Jackson

ELECTIONS

An election is coming. Universal peace is declared, and the foxes have a sincere interest in prolonging the lives of the poultry.

George Eliot

Our municipal elections run true to political form. The sewer was defeated but the councilmen got in.

Will Rogers

Elections are really a good deal like marriages, there's no accounting for anyone's taste. Every time you see a bridegroom, we wonder why she picked him, and it's the same with public officials.

Will Rogers

Anyone can be elected once by accident. Beginning with the second term, it's worth paying attention.

Sam Rayburn

Elections are won by men and women chiefly because most people vote against somebody, rather than for somebody.

Franklin P. Adams

Where the annual elections end, there slavery begins.

John Adams

Those who stay away from the election think that one vote will do no good: 'Tis but one step more to think one vote will do no harm.

Ralph Waldo Emerson

An elected official is one who gets 51 percent of the vote cast by 40 percent of the 60 percent of the voters who are registered.

Dan Bennett

Act as if the whole election depended on your single vote, and as if the whole Parliament (and therein the whole nation) on the single person whom you now choose to be a member of it.

John Wesley

Democracy's ceremonial, its feast, its great function, is the election.

H.G. Wells

An election is a moral horror, as bad as a battle except for the blood; a mud bath for every soul concerned in it.

George Bernard Shaw

I hate elections, but you have to have them—they are medicine.

Stanley Baldwin

77

The election is over, the results are now known;
The will of the people has been plainly shown;
So let's be friends and let differences pass,
I'll hug your elephant and you kiss my ass.

Frances Matthews

An election is a bet on the future, not a popularity contest of the past.

James Reston

ENEMIES

Love your enemies. It makes them so damned mad.

P.D. East

Speak well of your friend, of your enemy saying nothing.

Eighteenth-century proverb

Friends may come and go, but enemies accumulate.

Anonymous

Life'd not be worth livin' if we didn't keep our inimies.

Finley Peter Dunne

Cicero is reported to have been referring to Julius Caesar when he made the following statement:

He is his own worst enemy.

Bergen Evans—in his *Dictionary of Quotations*—writes:

It is said when the above saying was applied in his hearing to someone whom Sir Winston Churchill disliked, he quipped: "Not while I live."

In politics . . . you need two things: friends, but above all an enemy.

Brian Mulroney

ENTHUSIASM

Every great and commanding moment in the annals of the world is the triumph of some enthusiasm.

Ralph Waldo Emerson

It is unfortunate, considering that enthusiasm moves the world, that so few enthusiasts can be trusted to speak the truth.

Arthur Balfour

I used to be indecisive, but now I'm not so sure.

Boscoe Pertwee

EXPERTS

Always listen to experts. They'll tell you what can't be done and why. Then do it.

Robert A. Heinlein

An expert is a man who has made all the mistakes which can be made, in a very narrow field.

Niels Bohr

An expert is a man who avoids the small errors as he sweeps on to the grand fallacy.

Benjamin Stolberg

Someone from back east who knows exactly how much dynamite to stick up a bull's rump to blow off his horns without making his eyes water.

Mike Rosser

I want you to meet Blackstone the Magician, who has been teaching me the recondite art of prestidigitation or legerdemain. I can learn something from Mr. Blackstone, but I can assure you I can never learn anything from banks.

James Michael Curley

You don't set a fox to watching the chickens just because he has a lot of experience in the hen house.

Harry S.Truman

EXTREMISM

At the extreme of the political spectrum one encounters people who are moved chiefly to find an outlet for the venom that is in them.

D. Sutten

Extreme views are never just; something always turns up which disturbs the calculations formed upon their data.

Benjamin Disraeli

Every political good carried to the extreme must be productive of evil.

Mary Wollstonecraft

Political extremism involves two prime ingredients: an excessively simple diagnosis of the world's ills and a conviction that there are identifiable villains back of it all.

John Gardner

What is objectionable, what is dangerous about extremists is not that they are extreme, but that they are intolerant. The evil is not what they say about their cause, but what they say about their opponents.

Robert F. Kennedy

I would remind you that extremism in the defense of liberty is no vice. And let me remind you that moderation in the pursuit of justice is no virtue.

Barry Goldwater

FACTS

Oh, don't tell me of facts—I never believe facts; you know Canning said nothing was so fallacious as facts, except figures.

Sydney Smith

I don't write fiction. I invent facts.

Jorge Luis Borges

A beautiful theory, killed by a nasty, ugly, little fact.

Thomas Huxley

Get your facts first, and then you can distort them as much as you please.

Mark Twain

We do not deal much in facts when we are contemplating ourselves.

Mark Twain

You can't make the Duchess of Windsor into Rebecca of Sunnybrook Farm. The facts of life are very stubborn things.

Cleveland Amory

FAME

Woe unto you, when all men shall speak well of you!

Luke 6:26

THE WIT AND WISDOM OF POLITICS

Fame: the advantage of being known to those who do not know us.
Nicholas Chamfort

We are more solicitous that men speak of us, than how they speak.
Michel de Montaigne

Popularity is a crime from the moment it is sought; it is only a virtue where men have it whether they will or not.
George Savile

The temple of fame is the shortest passage to riches and preferment.
Junius

... Fame is like a shaved pig with a greased tail, and it is only after it has slipped through the hands of some thousands, that some fellow, by mere chance, holds on to it.
Davy Crockett

Fame is proof that the people are gullible.
Ralph Waldo Emerson

Some are born great, some achieve greatness, and some hire public relations writers.
Daniel Boorstin

He was a power politically for years, but he never got prominent enough to have his speeches garbled.
Frank McKinney Hubbard

We allow no man to tower over us. Won way or another we level th' wurruld to our height. If we can't reach th' heros' head we cut off his legs.
Finley Peter Dunne

You probably wouldn't worry about what people think of you if you could know how seldom they do.
Olin Miller

Fame is a comic distinction shared by Roy Roger's horse and Miss Watermelon of 1955.
Anonymous

Her greatest strength is she has never aspired to be popular. She has never wanted to be loved. . . . If you want to be loved, you are dead in the water. As soon as you come across a difficult thing, you will want to be loved and you won't do your duty.
Unidentified aide to Margaret Thatcher

The bad news is that one third of the people think I'm the banker who foreclosed on their farm, one third think I run the oil company that raised the price of gasoline and one third think I'm the guy who sold Manhattan to the Japanese.

Jay Rockefeller

FANATICISM/FANATICS

Fanatics seldom laugh. They never laugh at themselves.

James Gillis

A fanatic is one who sticks to his guns whether they're loaded or not.

Franklin P. Jones

A fanatic is one who can't change his mind and won't change the subject.

Winston S. Churchill

The worst vice of the fanatic is his sincerity.

Oscar Wilde

A fanatic is a man that does what he thinks th' Lord wud do if He knew th' facts iv th' case.

Finley Peter Dunne

Just as every conviction begins as a whim so does every emancipator serve his apprenticeship as a crank. A fanatic is a great leader who is just entering the room.

Heywood Broun

Fanaticism consists in redoubling your effort when you have forgotten your aim.

George Santayana

Fanaticism, the false fire of an overheated mind.

William Cowper

There is no place in a fanatic's head where reason can enter.

Napoleon Bonaparte

The less justified a man is in claiming experience for his own self, the more ready is he to claim all excellence for his nation, his religion, his race or his holy cause.

Eric Hoffer

The tendency to claim God as an ally for our partisan values and ends is . . . the source of all religious fanaticism.

Reinhold Niebuhr

Belief in a Divine mission is one of the many forms of certainty that have afflicted the human race.

Bertrand Russell

There is no arguing with the pretenders to a divine knowledge and to a divine mission. They are possessed with the sin of pride, they have yielded to perennial temptation.

Walter Lippmann

There is nobody as enslaved as a fanatic, the person in whom one impulse, one value, has assumed ascendency over all others.

Milton R. Saperstein

The worst government is the most moral. One composed of cynics is often very tolerant and humane. But when fanatics are on top there is no limit to oppression.

H.L. Mencken

Fanaticism is always a sign of repressed doubt.

Carl Gustav Jung

There is no strong performance without a little fanaticism in the performer.

Ralph Waldo Emerson

FILIBUSTERS

The senate filibustered. We pay for wisdom and get wind.

Will Rogers

During one filibuster one senator threatened to read the Bible into the Record, and I guess he would have done it, if somebody in the Capitol had had a Bible.

Will Rogers

Garner of Texas, Bascom Timmons' biography of John Nance Garner, tells of the time when Senator Huey Long was filibustering and asked Vice President Garner to require all senators to remain in the chamber to hear Long talk. Garner, who was not a fan of Long's, replied:

In the first place the Senator from Louisiana should not ask that. In the second place, it would be cruel and unusual punishment.

FLAGS

Many a bum show has been saved by the flag.

George M. Cohan

It seems like th' less a statesman amounts to, th' more he loves th' flag.

Frank McKinney Hubbard

Patriotic societies seem to think that the way to educate school children in democracy is to stage bigger and better flag saluting.

S.I. Hayakawa

Let us raise a standard to which the wise and honest can repair.

George Washington

The flag is the embodiment, not of sentiment, but of history. It represents the experiences made by men and women, the experiences of those who do and live under that flag.

Woodrow Wilson

A thoughtful mind, when it sees a nation's flag, sees not the flag only, but the nation itself, and whatever may be its symbols, its insignia, he reads chiefly in the flag the government, the principles, the truths, the history which belongs to the nation that sets it forth.

Henry Ward Beecher

Mark my words. It is only a matter of time before someone burns a flag, calls it "kinetic art" and gets a great grant to take his act on the road.

George Will

FREEDOM

The real value of freedom is not to the minority that wants to talk, but to the majority that does not want to listen.

Zechariah Chafee, Jr.

In our country we have those three unspeakably precious things: freedom of speech, freedom of conscience, and the prudence never to practice either.

Mark Twain

It is harder to preserve than obtain liberty.

John C. Calhoun

We want to be in control of our lives. Whether we are jungle fighters, craftsmen, company men, gamesmen, we want to be in control. And when the government erodes that control, we are not comfortable. We're not comfortable at all.

Barbara Jordan

We only want that which is given naturally to all peoples of the world, to be masters of our own fate, not of others, and in cooperation and friendship with others.

Golda Meir

We cannot defend freedom abroad by deserting it at home.

Edward R. Murrow

Necessity is the plea for every infringement of human freedom. It is the argument of tyrants; it is the creed of slaves.

William Pitt (the Elder)

No wait. I want to breathe the air of freedom in Moscow.

Mikhail Gorbachev

FRIENDS

God save me from my friends, I can protect myself from my enemies.

Marshal de Villars

A friend in power is a friend lost.

Henry Adams

In politics you must help your friends or you won't have any.

Russell Long

In prosperity it is very easy to find a friend, but in adversity it is the most difficult of all things.

Epictetus

Misfortune shows those who are not really friends.

Aristotle

Every good man looks after his friends, and any man who doesn't isn't likely to be popular.

George Washington Plunkitt

FUNERALS

He was retired too long. If you don't go to other people's funerals, they won't go to yours.

Chicago ward heeler
quoted in Time *magazine in 1946*

I did not attend his funeral, but I wrote a very nice letter saying that I approved of it.

Mark Twain

You all know me. I don't have to give a speech. Whenever you're going to need my services it'll be too late anyway.

County coroner in Gilpin County, Colorado

FUTURE

The trouble with our times is that the future is not what it used to be.

Paul Valéry

He who lives by the crystal ball soon learns to eat ground glass.

Anonymous

I resolve to be optimistic about the future—if there is one.

Anonymous

I have but one lamp by which my feet are guided, and that is the lamp of experience. I know no way of judging the future but by the past.

Patrick Henry

You can never plan the future by the past.

Edmund Burke

We should all be concerned about the future because we will have to spend the rest of our lives there.

Charles F. Kettering

I try to be as philosophical as the old lady who said that the best thing about the future is that it only comes one day at a time.

Dean Acheson

There is no way to understand the real options involved in the future unless you become involved in creating them.

Robert Theobald

I hold that man is in the right who is mostly in league with the future.
Henrik Ibsen

What do we want our kids to do? Sweep up around Japanese computers?
Walter Mondale

Life was meant to be lived, and curiosity must be kept alive. One must never, for whatever reason, turn his back on life.
Anna Eleanor Roosevelt

GOSSIP

If you haven't got something good to say about anyone, come and sit by me.
Alice Roosevelt Longworth

Gossip is when you hear something you like about someone you don't.
Earl Wilson

There is only one thing in the world worse than being talked about, and that is not being talked about.
Oscar Wilde

What some invent the rest enlarge.
Jonathan Swift

For prying into any human affairs, none are equal to those whom it does not concern.
Victor Hugo

Nothing is so swift as calumny; nothing is more easily uttered; nothing more readily received; nothing more widely dispersed.
Cicero

In Washington, gossip is intelligence.
Allan Gotlieb

GOVERNMENT

Thou dost not know, my son, with how little wisdom the world is governed.
Count Axel Oxenstierna

If it were not for the government, we should have nothing left to laugh at in France.

Nicholas Chamfort

The French

In general, the art of government consists in taking as much money as possible from one part of the citizens to give to the other.

Voltaire

If it is true that vice can never be done away with, the science of government consists of making it contribute to the public good.

Vauvenargues

Every country has the government it deserves.

Joseph de Maistre

To govern is to make choices.

Duc de Levis

The art of governing consists in not letting men grow old in their jobs.

Napoleon Bonaparte

How can you govern a country with two hundred and forty-six varieties of cheeses?

Charles de Gaulle

To govern is always to choose among disadvantages.

Charles de Gaulle

Every time the government attempts to handle our affairs, it costs more and the results are worse than if we had handled them ourselves.

Benjamin Constant

No government could survive without champagne. Champagne in the throats of our diplomatic people is like oil in the wheels of an engine.

Joseph Dargent

The British

It must be that to govern a nation you need a specific talent and that this may very well exist without general ability.

W. Somerset Maugham

THE WIT AND WISDOM OF POLITICS

I would not give half a guinea to live under one form of Government rather than another. It is of no moment to the happiness of an individual.

Samuel Johnson

The office of government is not to confer happiness, but to give men opportunity to work out happiness for themselves.

William Ellery Channing

Government is emphatically a machine; to the discontented a "taxing machine," to the contented a "machine for securing property."

Thomas Carlyle

It is with government as with medicine. Its only business is the choice of evils. Every law is an evil, for every law is an infraction of liberty.

Jeremy Bentham

Thou little thinkest what a little foolery governs the world.

John Selden

A faineant [lazy] government is not the worst government that England can have. It has been the great fault of our politicians that they have all wanted to do something.

Anthony Trollope

It is the duty of government to apply a great remedy to a great evil at all risks to themselves.

Lord John Russell

Of governments, that of the mob is most sanguinary, that of soldiers the most expensive, and that of civilians the most vexatious.

Charles Caleb Colton

I hardly know which is the greater pest to society, a paternal government—that is to say a prying, meddlesome government—which intrudes itself into every part of human life, and which thinks it can do everything for everybody better than anybody; or a careless, lounging government, which suffers grievances such as it could at once remove, and to which all complaint and remonstrance has only one answer: "We must let things alone; we must let things take their course; we must let things find their level." There is no more important problem in politics than to ascertain the just mean between these two most pernicious extremes, to draw correctly the line which divides those cases in which it is the duty of the State to interfere from those cases in which it is the duty of the State to abstain from interference.

Thomas B. Macaulay

He that goeth about to persuade a multitude that they are not so well governed as they ought to be, shall never want attentive and favorable hearers.

Richard Hooker

He that would govern others, first should be
The master of himself.

Philip Massinger

It would be desirable if every Government, when it comes into power, should have its old speeches burned.

Philip Snowden

The important thing for Government is not to do things which individuals are doing already, and to do them a little better or a little worse; but to do those things which at present are not done at all.

John Maynard Keynes

The whole duty of government is to prevent crime and to preserve contracts.

William Lamb (Lord Melbourne)

To prevent resentment, governments attribute misfortunes to natural causes; to create resentment, oppositions attribute them to human causes.

Bertrand Russell

The danger is not that a particular class is unfit to govern. Every class is unfit to govern.

Lord Acton

The Americans

The worst thing in this world, next to anarchy, is government.

Henry Ward Beecher

All government is evil, and the parent of evil. . . . The best government is that which governs least.

John O'Sullivan

The less government we have the better.

Ralph Waldo Emerson

I heartily accept the motto, "That government is best which governs least"; and I should like to see it acted up to more rapidly and systematically. Carried out, it finally amounts to this, which I also believe,—"That government is best which governs not at all."

Henry David Thoreau

Government expands to absorb revenue and then some.

Tom Wicker

Two characteristics of government are that it cannot do anything quickly, and that it never knows when to quit.

George Stigler

In government the sin of pride manifests itself in the recurring delusion that things are under control.

George Will

The ways of God and government and girls are all mysterious, and it is not given to mortal man to understand them.

Robert A. Heinlein

We send Democrats to Congress to get what we want, then send Republicans to the White House so we don't have to pay for it.

Tom Moloney

The Presidents

Government is not reason, it is not eloquence—it is force.

George Washington

The desire of the esteem of others is as real a want of nature as hunger. . . . It is a principal end of government to regulate this passion, which in its turn becomes a principal means of government. It is the only adequate instrument of order and subordination in society; and alone commands effectual obedience to laws, since without it neither human reason, nor standing armies, would ever produce that great effect.

John Adams

I am not a friend to a very energetic government. It is always oppressive. It places the government more at their ease, at the expense of the people.

Thomas Jefferson

What is government itself but the greatest of all reflections on human nature? If men were angels, no government would be necessary.

James Madison

All free governments are managed by the combined wisdom and folly of the people.

James A. Garfield

Though the people support the government, the government should not support the people.

Grover Cleveland

The government is us; we are the government, you and I.
Theodore Roosevelt

Whenever you have an efficient government you have a dictatorship.
Harry S. Truman

My experience in government is that when things are non-controversial, beautifully coordinated and all the rest, it must be that there is not much going on.
John F. Kennedy

No government is better than the men who compose it.
John F. Kennedy

Governments tend not to solve problems, only rearrange them.
Ronald Reagan

Government is not the solution to our problem. Government is the problem.
Ronald Reagan

My brother Bob doesn't want to be in government—he promised Dad he'd go straight.
John F. Kennedy

The trouble with us is that we talk about Jefferson but do not follow him. In his theory that the people should manage their government, and not be managed by it, he was everlastingly right.
Calvin Coolidge

The most terrifying words in the English language are, I'm from the government and I'm here to help.
Ronald Reagan

Other Views

Society in every state is a blessing, but government, even in its best state, is but a necessary evil, in its worst state an intolerable one.
Thomas Paine

Society is produced by our wants and government by our wickedness.
Thomas Paine

The very essence of a free government consists in considering offices as public trusts, bestowed for the good of the country, and not for the benefit of an individual or a party.
John C. Calhoun

For who are a free people? Not those over whom government is reasonably and equitably exercised, but those who live under a government so constitutionally checked and controlled, that proper provision is made against its being otherwise exercised.

John Dickinson

The final end of government is not to exert restraint but to do good.

Rufus Choate

Those who govern, having much business on their hands, do not generally like to take the trouble of considering and carrying into execution new projects. The best public measures are therefore seldom adopted from previous wisdom, but forced by the occasion.

Benjamin Franklin

Class and group divisions based on property lie at the basis of modern governments; and politics and constitutional law are inevitably a reflex of these contending interests.

Charles A. Beard

If our democracy is to flourish, it must have criticism; if our government is to function it must have dissent.

Henry Steele Commager

Popular government has not yet been proved to guarantee, always and everywhere, good government.

Walter Lippmann

It is a function of government to invent philosophies to explain the demands of its own convenience.

Murray Kempton

Government is too big and important to be left to the politicians.

Chester Bowles

I am against government by crony.

Harold Ickes

A government is the only known vessel that leaks from the top.

James Reston

Frankly, I'd like to see government get out of war altogether and leave the whole field to private industry.

Joseph Heller

Government is the political representative of a natural equilibrium, of custom, of inertia; it is by no means a representative of reason.

George Santayana

In a change of government, the poor seldom change anything except the name of their master.

Phaedrus

Oppressive government is more terrible than tigers.

Confucius

Life is a great and noble game between the citizen and the government. The government nearly always scores, but the citizen should not thereby be discouraged. Even if he always loses the game, it is in his power to inflict a considerable amount of annoyance on the victors.

Rose Macaulay

It is perfectly true that the government is best which governs least. It is equally true that the government is best which provides the most.

Walter Lippmann

To administer is to govern, to govern is to reign. That is the essence of the problem.

Honoré Gabriel Mirabeau

Th' older a guv'ment is, the better 't suits; new ones hunt folks' corns out like new boots.

James Russell Lowell

Even though counting heads is not an ideal way to govern, it is at least better than breaking them.

Learned Hand

No one can terrorize a whole nation unless we are all his accomplices.

Edward R. Murrow

Traditional autocrats . . . favor the affluent few and maintain masses in poverty.

Jeanne Kirkpatrick

The government is unpopular, but I'm popular.

Mikhail Gorbachev

But the establishment is made up of little men, very frightened.

Bella Abzug

HEALTH CARE

If criminals have a right to a lawyer, I think working Americans have a right to a doctor.

Harris Wofford

The bottom line on the public's attitude is: Spend whatever is needed for health care—particularly on me—just don't bill us for it.

Richard Morin

HISTORY

The study of history is the beginning of political wisdom.

Jean Bodin

What experience and history teach is this—that people and governments never have learned anything from history, or acted on principles deduced from it.

Hegel

Our ignorance of history causes us to slander our own times.

Gustave Flaubert

A generation which ignores history has no past—and no future.

Robert A. Heinlein

The more we know of history, the less shall we esteem the subjects of it, and to despise our species is the price we must too often pay for our knowledge of it.

Charles Caleb Colton

If men could learn from history, what lessons it might teach us! But passion and party blind our eyes, and the light which experience gives is a lantern on the stern, which shines only on the waves behind us!

Samuel Taylor Coleridge

What is history after all? History is facts which become lies in the end; legends are lies which become history in the end.

Jean Cocteau

We will hereafter believe less history than ever, now that we have seen how it is made.

Don Herold

History is the witness that testifies to the passing of time; it illumines reality, vitalizes memory, provides guidance in daily life, and brings us tidings of antiquity.

Cicero

Man is a history-making creature who can neither repeat his past nor leave it behind.

W.H. Auden

Historical phenomena always happen twice—the first time as tragedy, the second as farce.

Karl Marx

History is past politics, and politics is present history.

E.A. Freeman

History never repeats itself . . . historians repeat themselves.

Anonymous

History is largely concerned with arranging good entrances for people and later exits not always quite so good.

Heywood Broun

HONESTY

An honest politician is one who, when he is bought, will stay bought.

Simon Cameron

My idea of an honest man is a fellow who will pay income tax on the money he sold his vote for.

Will Rogers

Be frank and explicit. That is the right line to take, when you wish to conceal your own mind and to confuse the minds of others.

Benjamin Disraeli

Be yourself and speak your mind today, though it contradict all you have said before.

Elbert Hubbard

Always acknowledge a fault frankly. This will throw those in authority off their guard and give you opportunity to commit more.

Mark Twain

We confess to small faults only to convey the impression that we have no big ones.

La Rochefoucauld

A little confession isn't only good for the soul; it's also often good politics.

Vermont Royster

Few men have virtue to withstand the higher bidder.

George Washington

Every time the city built a school, a politician went into the real estate business.

Fiorello H. La Guardia

The city did not get what it paid for. Although it certainly paid for what it got.

Joseph D. McGoldrick

It [the speech] wasn't my finest hour. It wasn't even my finest hour and a half.

Bill Clinton

HONOR

I have often observed that nothing ever perplexes an adversary so much as an appeal to his honor.

Benjamin Disraeli

The louder he talked of his honor, the faster we counted our spoons.

Ralph Waldo Emerson

It is better to deserve honors and not to have them than to have them and not deserve them.

Mark Twain

HUMOR IN POLITICS

On a throne at the center of a sense of humor sits a capacity for irony. All wit rests on a cheerful awareness of life's incongruities. It is a gentling awareness, and no politician without it should be allowed near power.

George Will

Public men should take their jobs seriously, but not themselves.

Dean Acheson

To keep the machinery of government operating efficiently, it must be oiled frequently with fun and laughter; otherwise friction and hate will soon wear it out.

Tom Corwin

Never make people laugh. If you would succeed in life, you must be solemn, solemn as an ass. All great monuments are built over solemn asses.

Tom Corwin

In politics you've got to have a sense of humor. If you don't have humor you'll end up in a nuthouse with a host of paper dolls.

Michael Pendergast

A sense of humor covers up a lot of ill feelings. If you can't laugh at yourself and laugh with your friends, the bitterness of a battle never goes away. Your enemy of today has to be your ally of tomorrow.

John Vanderhoof

There's no trick to being a humorist when you have the whole government working for you.

Will Rogers

Man is the only animal that laughs. He's also the only animal that has a legislature.

Betty Ann Dittemore

Everything human is pathetic. The secret source of Humor itself is not joy but sorrow. There is no humor in heaven.

Mark Twain

I laugh because I must not cry. That is all. That is all.

Abraham Lincoln

If you lose the power to laugh, you lose the power to think.

Clarence Darrow

Men will confess to treason, murder, arson, false teeth, or a wig. How many of them will own up to a lack of humor?

Frank Moore Colby

The man who can make others laugh secures more votes for a measure than the man who forces them to think.

Malcolm de Chazal

THE WIT AND WISDOM OF POLITICS

Fortune and humor govern the world.

La Rochefoucauld

When the governed laugh, the governors cannot but have an uneasy feeling that they may well be laughing at them.

Malcolm Muggeridge

The monuments of wit survive the monuments of power.

Francis Bacon

My method is to take the utmost trouble to find the right thing to say, and then to say it with the utmost levity.

George Bernard Shaw

One of the most useful weapons in a Speaker's armory is a sense of humor and a wit which, if used in the correct way and at the right moment can bring the Commons to heel like a hunting horn with a pack of hounds.

Hugh Noyes

I found that four fifths of the House were composed of country squires and great fools; my first effort, therefore, was by a lively sally, or an ironical remark to make them laugh; that laugh effaced the recollection of what had been urged in opposition to my view of the subject from their stupid pates and then I shipped in an argument, and had all the way clear before me.

Richard Brinsley Sheridan

If wit in American politics is less frequent, less subtle, and more heavy-handed, this may also be due to the higher incidence of lawyers in the American legislatures.

Leon A. Harris

Politics should be fun, politicians have no right to be dull or po-faced. The moment politics becomes dull, democracy is in danger.

Lord Hailsham

He who laughs, lasts.

Mary Pettibone Poole

We are all here for a spell, get all the good laughs you can.

Anonymous

If a presidential candidate is lacking in humor then forget him, don't vote for him. He lacks the presidential sensibility ... he'll never succeed with Congress, or rally the will of the people.

Peggy Noonan

The world is so overflowing with absurdity that it is difficult for the humorist to compete.

Malcolm Muggeridge

The politician is an educator, and his first responsibility is to educate the public, and one of the techniques of education is to tickle their fancy and their sense of humor.

Adlai Stevenson

HYPOCRISY

A hypocrite is the kind of politician who would cut down a redwood tree, then mount the stump and make a speech for conservation.

Adlai Stevenson

Man is no angel. He is sometimes more of a hypocrite and sometimes less, and then fools say that he has or has not principles.

Honoré de Balzac

Hypocrisy can afford to be magnificent in its promises; for never intending to go beyond promises, it costs nothing.

Edmund Burke

IDEALISM/IDEALISTS

I am an idealist. I don't know where I'm going but I'm on my way.

Carl Sandburg

Idealism is the noble toga that political gentlemen drape over their will to power.

Aldous Huxley

Idealists may have their faults, but they rarely steal.

Arthur M. Schlesinger, Jr.

When they come down from their Ivory Towers, Idealists are very apt to work straight into the gutter.

Logan Pearsall Smith

I thought what an awful thing is idealism when reality is so marvelous.

Joanna Field

THE WIT AND WISDOM OF POLITICS

The test of an ideal or rather of an idealist, is the power to hold to it and get one's inspiration from it under difficulties. When one is comfortable and well off, it is easy to talk high.

Oliver Wendell Holmes, Jr.

Idealism increases in direct proportion to one's distance from the problem.

John Galsworthy

An ideal is often but a flaming vision of reality.

Joseph Conrad

Idealism is fine; but as it approaches reality, the cost becomes prohibitive.

William F. Buckley, Jr.

If you are not an idealist by the time you are twenty you don't have a heart, but if you are still an idealist by thirty you don't have a head.

Randolph Bourne

Our ideals, like the gods of old, are constantly demanding human sacrifices.

George Bernard Shaw

Every dogma has its day, but ideals are eternal.

Israel Zangwill

Nothing is more dangerous than a disillusioned idealist.

Johann Wolfgang von Goethe

Sometimes people call me an idealist. Well, that is the way I know I am an American. America is the only idealistic nation in the world.

Woodrow Wilson

There is nothing the matter with Americans except their ideals. The real American is all right; it is the ideal American who is all wrong.

G.K. Chesterton

Ideals are like stars: you will not succeed in touching them with your hands, but like the seafaring man on the desert of waters, you choose them as your guides, and following them you reach your destiny.

Carl Schurz

Each time a man stands up for an ideal, or acts to improve the lot of others, or strikes out against injustice, he sends forth a tiny ripple of hope

...and crossing each other from a million different centers of energy and daring those ripples build a current that can sweep down the mightiest walls of oppression and resistance.

Robert F. Kennedy

IDEAS

The public doesn't require any new ideas. The public is best served by the good, old-fashioned ideas it already has.

Henrik Ibsen

A mind that is stretched to a new idea never returns to its original dimension.

Oliver Wendell Holmes

An invasion of armies can be resisted, but not an idea whose time has come.

Victor Hugo

There is nothing more difficult to take in hand, more perilous to conduct, or more uncertain in its success, than to take the lead in the introduction of a new order of things.

Niccolò Machiavelli

Let a man proclaim a new principle. Public sentiment will surely be on the other side.

Thomas B. Reed

The human mind treats a new idea the way the body treats a strange protein; it rejects it.

Sir Peter Brian Medawar

One of the greatest pains to human nature is the pain of a new idea.

Walter Bagehot

New opinions are always suspected, and usually opposed, without any other reason but they are not already common.

John Locke

An important scientific innovation rarely makes its way by gradually winning over and converting its opponents; it rarely happens that Saul becomes Paul. What does happen is that its opponents gradually die out and that the growing generation is familiarized with the idea from the beginning.

Max Planck

Let's remind ourselves that last year's fresh idea is today's cliche.

Austen Briggs

The vitality of thought is in adventure. Ideas won't keep. Something must be done about them. When the idea is new, its custodians have fervor, live for it, and, if need be, die for it.

Alfred North Whitehead

An idea that is not dangerous is unworthy of being called an idea at all.

Elbert Hubbard

New ideas are for the most part like bad sixpences, and we spend our lives trying to pass them off on one another.

Samuel Butler (poet)

For an idea ever to be fashionable is ominous, since it must afterward be always old-fashioned.

George Santayana

No matter what occurs, there is always someone who believes it happened according to his pet theory.

Anonymous

IGNORANCE

The trouble ain't that people are ignorant; it's that they know so much that ain't so.

Josh Billings

Nothing is more terrible than ignorance in action.

Johann Wolfgang von Goethe

Nothing is as awesome as ignorance in action.

Betty Ann Dittemore

Ignorance never settles a question.

Benjamin Disraeli

INDEPENDENT VOTERS

An independent is the guy who wants to take the politics out of politics.

Adlai Stevenson

Unless some one is partisan no one can be an independent.

Calvin Coolidge

When people—particularly scholars—say they are nonpolitical and impartial, what they usually mean is that they are successfully middle-class.

Dr. Alex Comfort

INFLATION

Inflation is like sin; every government denounces it and every government practices it.

Sir Frederick Leith-Ross

The first panacea for a mismanaged nation is inflation of the currency;
the second is war. Both bring a temporary prosperity; both bring a
permanent ruin. But both are the refuge of political and economic
opportunists.

Ernest Hemingway

There's only one place where inflation is made: that's in Washington...in
response to pressures from the people at large.... The voting public...ask
their Congressmen to enact goodies in the form of spending, but they are
unhappy about having taxes raised to pay for those goodies.

Milton Friedman

INFLUENCE

Influence: a power you think you have until you try to use it.

Anonymous

Influence is like a savings account. The less you use it, the more you've got.

Andrew Young

Influence, n.
In politics, a visionary quo given in exchange for a substantial quid.

Ambrose Bierce

INTELLECTUALS

You hear a lot of talk about the Tammany district leaders being illiterate
men. If illiterate means havin' common sense, we plead guilty. But if
they mean that the Tammany leaders ain't go no education and ain't
gents, they don't know what they're talkin' about. Of course, we ain't
all bookworms and professors. If we were, Tammany might win an
election once in four thousand years. We've got bookworms too, in the
organization. But we don't make them district leaders. We keep them
for ornaments on parade days.

George Washington Plunkitt

The misfortune of high-minded intellectuals [in politics] is that, until it is too late, they remain as unaware of the sudden waves of emotion by which the majority can be swayed as they do of the shabby secret stratagems of ambitious men.

Sir Harold Nicolson

Who—except a freakish intellectual—has ever been argued into giving up political power when he doesn't have to; and to give it up, moreover, for the sake of an abstraction, a principle? The idea is ludicrous.

Julian Barnes

That's so silly only an intellectual would believe it.

Anonymous

An intellectual is someone who thinks saying it is the same as doing it.

Dan Buck

An intellectual is a man who takes more words than necessary to tell more than he knows.

Dwight David Eisenhower

INVESTIGATIONS

Our investigations have always contributed more to amusement than they have to knowledge.

Will Rogers

I don't care who you are, you just can't reach middle life without having done and said a whole lot of foolish things. If I saw an investigating committee headed my way, I would just plead guilty, and throw myself on the mercy of the court.

Will Rogers

If Congress would only hang somebody, no matter if they were guilty or not, just for an example, why, we could forgive them for all their investigations.

Will Rogers

ISSUES

The man who raises new issues has always been distasteful to politicians. He musses up what had been so tidily arranged.

Walter Lippman

Issues are like snakes—they just refuse to die! They keep coming back, time after time.

Howard Baker

We're all fuzzy on the issues. That's proven by the fact that we did get elected. The advantage of being a presidential candidate is that you have a much broader range of issues on which to be fuzzy.

James Earl Carter, Jr.

I don't know anything about free silver. The people of Nebraska are for free silver and I am for free silver. I will look up the arguments later.

William Jennings Bryan

There are no issues. My opponent has a job and I want it. That's what this election is about.

William J. Bulow

J

JUDGES/JUDICIAL

A judge who seeks political office insults his robes.

Andrew Jackson

Seldom in doubt, frequently in error.

Old legal proverb

There is hardly a political question in the United States which does not sooner or later turn into a judicial one.

Alexis de Tocqueville

The acme of judicial distinction means the ability to look a lawyer straight in the eye for two hours and not hear a damned word he says.

John Marshall

The mark of a good judge is a judge whose opinion you can read and have no idea if the judge was a man or woman, Republican or Democrat, a Christian or a Jew and, if a Christian, a Protestant or a Catholic. You just know he or she was a good judge.

Potter Stewart

Judges are but men, and in all ages have shown a fair share of frailty. Alas! Alas! The worst crimes of history have been perpetrated under their sanction, the blood of martyrs and patriots, crying from the ground, summons them to judgment.

Charles Sumner

Judges . . . are picked out from the most dexterous lawyers, who are grown old or lazy, and having been biassed all their lives against truth and equity are under such a fatal necessity of favoring fraud, perjury and oppression, that I have known several of them refuse a large bribe from the side where justice lay, rather than injure the faculty by doing anything unbecoming their nature or their office.

Jonathan Swift

When the state court judge puts on his or her federal court robe, he or she does not become immediately better equipped intellectually to do the job.

Sandra Day O'Connor

A judge I helped elect was mugged recently. And do you know what he did? He called a press conference and said: "This mugging of me will in no way affect my decisions in matters of this kind." And an elderly lady got up in the back of the room and said: "Then mug him again."

Ed Koch

Judicial reform is no sport for the short-winded.

Arthur Vanderbilt

Judges . . . rule on the basis of law, not public opinion, and they should be totally indifferent to pressures of the times.

Warren E. Burger

JUDGMENT

Good judgment is frequently the result of experience and experience is frequently the result of bad judgment.

Robert Lovett

The trouble is, we judge ourselves by our motives and others by their actions.

Dwight Morrow

All general judgments are loose and imperfect.

Michel de Montaigne

I pass with relief from the tossing sea of Cause and Theory to the firm ground of Result and Fact.

Winston S. Churchill

JUSTICE

Injustice is relatively easy to bear; it is justice that hurts.

H.L. Mencken

The love of justice in most men is nothing more than the fear of suffering injustice.

La Rochefoucauld

A jury consists of twelve persons chosen to decide who has the better lawyer.

Robert Frost

Injustice anywhere is a threat to justice everywhere.

Martin Luther King

Under the right prosecutor, a grand jury would indict a ham sandwich.

Anonymous

Justice delayed is democracy denied.

Robert F. Kennedy

K

KNOWLEDGE

Nothing is so firmly believed as that which we least know.

Michel de Montaigne

It is better to know nothing than to know what ain't so.

Josh Billings

Better know nothing than half-know many things.

Nietzsche

When you know a thing, to hold that you know it; and when you do not know a thing, to allow that you do not know it—that is knowledge.

Confucius

LABELS

Labels are an attempt to substitute slogans for thought.

Nelson Rockefeller

Labels are for cans, not for people.

Anonymous

LAW
There are two things you don't want to watch being made; one is sausages; the other is laws.

Anonymous

The less people know about how sausages and laws are made, the better they'll sleep at night.

Otto von Bismarck

The Greeks
Good laws, if they are not obeyed, do not constitute good government.

Aristotle

The habit of changing laws lightly is an evil.

Aristotle

Musical innovation is full of danger to the State, for when modes of music change, the laws of the State always change with them.

Plato

Nobody has a more sacred obligation to obey the law than those who make the law.

Sophocles

Law stands mute in the midst of arms.

Cicero

The more corrupt the state, the more numerous the laws.

Tacitus

Some laws, though unwritten, are more firmly established than all written laws.

Seneca

The French
There is no man so good, who, were he to submit all his thoughts and actions to the laws, would not deserve hanging ten times in his life.

Michel de Montaigne

Let all the laws be clear, uniform, and precise; to interpret laws is almost always to corrupt them.

Voltaire

Good laws lead to the making of better ones; bad ones bring about worse.

Jean-Jacques Rousseau

'Tis easier to make certain things legal than to make them legitimate.

Nicholas Chamfort

The majestic egalitarianism of the law, which forbids rich and poor alike to sleep under bridges, to beg in the streets, and to steal bread.

Anatole France

The British

There is more learning required to explain a law than went into the making of it.

George Savile

The law hath so many contradictions, and varyings from itself that the law may not improperly be called a lawbreaker.

George Savile

The law is a sort of hocus pocus science.

Charles Macklin

"If the law supposes that," said Mr. Bumble . . . "the law is an ass, an idiot."

Charles Dickens

The wisdom of a lawmaker consisteth not only in a platform of justice, but in the application thereof.

Francis Bacon

Ignorance of the law excuses no man; not that all men know the law, but because 'tis an excuse every man will plead, and no man can tell how to refute him.

John Selden

How small, of all that human hearts endure,
That part which kings or laws can cause or cure!

Samuel Johnson

Laws were made to be broken.

Christopher North

Where laws end, tyranny begins.

William Pitt (the Younger)

Bad laws are the worst sort of tyranny.

Edmund Burke

The Law of England is a very strange one; it cannot compel anyone to tell the truth. . . . But what the Law can do is to give you seven years for not telling the truth.

Charles John Darling

Men would be great criminals did they need as many laws as they make.

Charles John Darling

When you break the big laws, you do not get liberty; you do not even get anarchy. You get the small laws.

G.K. Chesterton

We do not get good laws to restrain bad people. We get good people to restrain bad laws.

G.K. Chesterton

The Americans

. . . It will be of little avail . . . if the laws are so voluminous that they cannot be read, or so incoherent that they cannot be understood . . . or undergo such incessant changes that no man who knows the law today can guess what it will be tomorrow.

The Federalist Papers

The United States is the greatest law factory the world has ever known.

Charles Evans Hughes

If there isn't a law, there will be.

Harold Faber

If you laid all our laws end to end, there would be no end.

"Bugs" Baer

Fidelity to the public requires that the law be as plain and as explicit as possible, that the less knowing may understand, and not be ensnared by them, while the artful evade their force.

Samuel Cooke

Of course there's a different law for the rich and the poor; otherwise, who would go into business?

E. Ralph Stewart

People say law, but they mean wealth.

Ralph Waldo Emerson

Most laws are passed because of "people who want to do good and people who want to do well."

Milton Friedman

The law isn't justice. It's a very imperfect mechanism. If you press exactly the right buttons and are also lucky, justice may also turn up in the answer.

Raymond Chandler

Laws too gentle are seldom obeyed; too severe, seldom executed.

Benjamin Franklin

I know no method to secure the repeal of bad or obnoxious laws so effective as their stringent execution.

Ulysses S. Grant

I sometimes wish that people would put a little more emphasis upon the observance of law than they do upon its enforcement.

Calvin Coolidge

The people have nothing to do with the laws but to obey them.

Edgar Allan Poe

Law never made men a whit more just.

Henry David Thoreau

It usually takes a hundred years to make a law, and then, after it has done its work, it usually takes a hundred years to get rid of it.

Henry Ward Beecher

With Congress, every time they make a joke it's a law; and every time they make a law it's a joke.

Will Rogers

It ain't no sin if you crack a few laws now and then, just as long as you don't break any.

Mae West

A law can be both economic folly and constitutional.

Antonin Scalia

The following appear as "Oaks' Unruly Laws for Lawmakers" in the Congregational Record:

- Bad law is more likely to be supplemented than repealed.

- Law expands in proportion to the resources available for its enforcement.

- Bad or complicated law tends to drive out good judgment.

- An uninformed lawmaker is more likely to produce a complicated law than a simple one.

Other Views

Laws are spider webs through which the big flies pass and the little ones get caught.

Honoré de Balzac

The greater the number of laws and enactments, the more thieves and robbers there will be.

Lao-tzu

I have spent all my life under a Communist regime, and I will tell you that a society without an objective legal scale is a terrible one indeed. But a society with no other scale but the legal one is not quite worthy of man either.

Alexander Solzhenitsyn

In Germany, under the law everything is prohibited except that which is permitted. In France, under the law everything is permitted except that which is prohibited. In the Soviet Union, everything is prohibited, including that which is permitted. And in Italy, under the law everything is permitted, especially that which is prohibited.

Newton Minow

LAWSUITS

Avoid lawsuits beyond all things; they influence your conscience, impair your health, and dissipate your property.

La Bruyère

I never was ruined but twice. Once when I lost a lawsuit and once when I won one.

Voltaire

If you have a strong case in law, talk to the judge. If you have a strong case in fact, talk to the jury. But if you have no case in law or fact, talk to the wild elements and bellow like a bull.

Joe Baldwin

When you're weak on facts , argue the law. When you're weak on the law, argue the facts. When you're weak on both the law and the facts, you attack the prosecution.

Old adage

When you have no basis for an argument, abuse the plaintiff.

Cicero

LAWYERS

Woe unto you also, ye lawyers! for ye lade men with burdens grievous to be borne, and ye yourselves touch not the burdens with one of your "fingers."

Luke 11:46

They have no lawyers among them, for they consider them as a sort of people whose profession it is to disguise matters.

Sir Thomas More

The first thing we do, let's kill all the lawyers.

William Shakespeare

It is likewise to be observed that this society (of lawyers) hath a particular chant and jargon of their own, that no other mortal can understand, and wherein all their laws are written, which they take special care to multiply; whereby they have wholly confounded the very essence of truth and falsehood.

Jonathan Swift

If the laws could speak for themselves they would complain of lawyers in the first place.

George Savile

It is a maxim among lawyers, that whatever hath been done before may legally be done again: and therefore they take special care to record all the decisions formerly made against common justice and the general reason of mankind. These, under the name of precedents, they produce as authorities, to justify the most iniquitous opinions: and the judges never fail of directing accordingly.

Jonathan Swift

I think we may class the lawyer in the natural history of monsters.

John Keats

Lawyers are the only persons in whom ignorance of the law is not punished.

Jeremy Bentham

THE WIT AND WISDOM OF POLITICS

A lawyer's opinion is worth nothing unless paid for.

English proverb

Always remember that when you go into an attorney's office door, you will have to pay for it, first or last.

Anthony Trollope

A lawyer is a learned gentleman who rescues your estate from your enemies and keeps it for himself.

Lord Brougham

He did not care to speak ill of any man behind his back, but he believed the gentleman was an attorney.

Samuel Johnson

He is no lawyer who cannot take two sides.

Charles Lamb

It is hard to say whether the doctors of law or divinity have made the greatest advances in the lucrative business of mystery.

Edmund Burke

A lawyer's dream of heaven—every man reclaimed his property at the resurrection, and each tried to recover it from all his forefathers.

Samuel Butler (poet)

When lawyers talk about the law, the normal human being begins to think about something else.

Richard Ingrams

"In my youth," said his father, "I took to the law,
And argued each case with my wife;
And the muscular strength which it gave my jaw
Has lasted the rest of my life."

Lewis Carroll

If there were no bad people there would be no good lawyers.

Charles Dickens

Lawyers and painters can soon change white to black.

Danish proverb

[Lawyers are] . . . savage beasts of prey who moved in swarms.

The men in Shay's Rebellion

God works wonders now and then;
Behold! a lawyer, an honest man
Benjamin Franklin

Necessity knows no law: I know some attorneys of the same.
Benjamin Franklin

Their nature, by training and instinct, is to argue and procrastinate. Yet we persist in electing lawyers to Congress.
Benjamin Franklin (attr.)

It is the trade of lawyers to question everything, yield nothing, and to talk by the hour.
Thomas Jefferson

The lawyer tries to take advantage of bad laws. The politician—or rather the statesman—tries to bring about the adoption of good laws.
Thomas Jefferson

Discourage litigation. Persuade your neighbors to compromise whenever you can.... As a peacemaker the lawyer has a superior opportunity of being a good man. There will still be business enough.
Abraham Lincoln

I used to be a lawyer, but now I am a reformed character.
Woodrow Wilson

Lawyers take to politics like bears take to honey.
Robert Townsend

The undertaker politicians and the saloon-keeper politicians have given way to lawyer-politicians ... who are no better ... and they don't ever buy you a drink or offer a prayer.
Mike Royko

Our politics is rotten because it is almost exclusively made up of lawyers.
Jimmy Breslin

I have concluded in my old age that the city [Washington] is too full of two kinds of people: lawyers and press people. It is quite clear now that the lawyers paralyze everything. That's what lawyers are for, to keep things from happening.
Eric Sevareid

Most good lawyers live well, work hard, and die poor.
Daniel Webster

THE WIT AND WISDOM OF POLITICS

A lawyer starts life giving five hundred dollars' worth of law for five dollars and ends up giving five dollars' worth for five hundred dollars.

Benjamin H. Brewster

A man may as well open an oyster without a knife, as a lawyer's mouth without a fee.

Barten Holyday

Lawyers, ah yes, they have courage. But only when it is time to send the bill.

J.P. Donleavy

Ignorance of the law does not prevent the losing lawyer from collecting his bill.

Puck magazine

Lawyer—one who protects us us against robbers by taking away the temptation.

H.L. Mencken

Two lawyers can live in a town where one cannot.

V.S. Lean

Three Philadelphia lawyers are a match for the Devil.

H.L. Mencken (attr.)

Too often lawyers are men who turn poetry into prose and prose into jargon.

John Maynard Keynes

The lawyer's truth is not Truth, but consistency or a consistent expediency.

Henry David Thoreau

What is a stone wall to a layman is a triumphal arch to a corporation lawyer.

Finley Peter Dunne

Lawyers are people with delusions of adequacy.

Robert Emmit Cox

Insects, weeds and lawyers will inherit the earth.

Olin Webb

What do lawyers and prostitutes have in common? If the fee is right they'll assume any position.

Anonymous

The trouble with law is lawyers.

Clarence Darrow

Lawyers spend a great deal of their time shoveling smoke.

Oliver Wendell Holmes, Jr.

To some lawyers, all facts are created equal.

Felix Frankfurter

Law school taught me one thing: how to take two situations that are exactly the same and show how they are different.

Hart Pomerantz (attr.)

I don't want a lawyer to tell me what I cannot do; I hire him to tell me how to do what I want to do.

J. Pierpont Morgan

You never get into trouble attacking lawyers. Everyone ought to take every opportunity to bash lawyers. It's so easy.

Marlin Fitzwater

LEADERSHIP

A leader should not get too far in front of his troops or he will get shot in the ass.

Joseph S. Clark

To be a leader of men one must turn one's back on men.

Havelock Ellis

Look over your shoulder now and then to be sure someone's following you.

Henry Gilmer

To lead the people, walk behind them.

Lao-tzu

In democracies, those who lead, follow; those who follow, lead.

Holbrook Jackson

I must follow the people. Am I not their leader?

Benjamin Disraeli

If I advance, follow me! If I retreat, kill me! If I die, avenge me!

La Rochejacquelein

THE WIT AND WISDOM OF POLITICS

The men who have changed the universe have never accomplished it by changing officials but always by inspiring the people.

Napoleon Bonaparte

A leader is a dealer in hope.

Napoleon Bonaparte

As soon as you are complicated, you are ineffectual.

Konrad Adenauer

A leader who doesn't hesitate before he sends his nation into battle is not fit to be a leader.

Golda Meir

A leader or a man of action in a crisis almost always acts subconsciously and then thinks of the reasons for his action.

Jawaharlal Nehru

The first function of a political leader is advocacy. It is he who must make articulate the wants, the frustration, and the aspiration of the masses.

Aneurin Bevan

Those who want to lead must never hesitate about sacrificing their friends.

Benjamin Disraeli

Because a man is what is called leader of a party, does that constitute him a censor and a judge of faith and morals? I will not accept it. It would make life intolerable.

William Gladstone

There is no worse mistake in public leadership than to hold out false hopes soon to be swept away.

Winston S. Churchill

I am certainly not one of those who need to be prodded. In fact, if anything, I am the prod.

Winston S. Churchill

I see it said that leaders should keep their ears to the ground. All I can say is that the British nation will find it very hard to look up to leaders who are detected in that somewhat ungainly posture. o

Winston S. Churchill

A true leader always keeps an element of surprise up his sleeve, which others cannot grasp but which keeps his public excited and breathless.

Charles de Gaulle

Every man of action has a strong dose of egotism, pride, hardness and cunning. But all those things will be forgiven him, indeed, they will be regarded as high dualities, if he can make them the means to achieve great ends.

Charles de Gaulle

A prime function of leadership is to combine the "thoughts and feelings" of "the common mind" into acts of recognition and completion.

Woodrow Wilson

It is harder for a leader to be born in a palace than to be born in a cabin.

Woodrow Wilson

A leader has to lead, or otherwise he has no business in politics.

Harry S. Truman

Men make history and not the other way around. In periods where there is no leadership, society stands still. Progress occurs when courageous, skillful leaders seize the opportunity to change things for the better.

Harry S. Truman

I would rather try to persuade a man to go along, because once I have persuaded him he will stick. If I scare him, he will stay just as long as he is scared, and then he is gone.

Dwight David Eisenhower

Leadership and learning are indispensable to each other.

John F. Kennedy

A mean streak is a very important quality of leadership.

Charles E. Goodell

Charlatanism of some degree is indispensable to effective leadership.

Eric Hoffer

The real leader has no need to lead—he is content to point the way.

Henry Miller

Leadership appears to be the art of getting others to want to do something you are convinced should be done.

Vance Packard

You take people as far as they will go, not as far as you would like them to go.

Jeanette Rankin

THE WIT AND WISDOM OF POLITICS

The leader must know, must know that he knows, and must be able to make it abundantly clear to those around him that he knows.

Clarence B. Randall

Those who govern most make the least noise.

John Sidden

Defeat in itself was part and parcel of the great gambling game of politics. A man who could not accept it and try again was not of the stuff of which leaders are made.

Agnes Sligh Turnbull

Where there is no vision the people perish.

Proverb

He who has never learned to obey cannot be a good commander.

Aristotle

It is frequently a misfortune to have very brilliant men in charge of affairs; they expect too much of ordinary men.

Thucydides

In the case of political, and even religious leaders it is often very doubtful whether they have done more good or harm.

Albert Einstein

A leader is one who, out of madness or goodness, volunteers to take upon himself the woe of a people. There are few men so foolish, hence the erratic quality of leadership in the world.

John Updike

The emperor sent his troops into the field with immense enthusiasm; he will lead them in person—when they return.

Mark Twain

No labor leader can deliver the vote. If any labor leader says he can deliver the vote he is kidding you or himself. He can influence and try to mobilize his people around issues, and they will deliver the vote.

Walter Reuther

A leader is best
When people barely know he exists
Not so good when people obey and acclaim him,
Worse when they despise him.
"Fail to honor people,

They fail to honor you";
But of a good leader, who talks little,
When his work is done, his aim fulfilled,
They will say, "We did this ourselves."

Lao-tzu

The cause is strong which has not a multitude, but one strong man behind it.

James Russell Lowell

If you approach people the right way, you could get them to applaud their own hanging.

Unidentified political analyst

De Gaulle did not call in "writers"; the very idea is grotesque. The leader who allows others to speak for him is abdicating.

May Sarton

If you doubt you can accomplish something, then you can't accomplish it. You have to have confidence in your ability, and then be tough enough to follow through.

Rosalynn Carter

You don't lead a crusade with question marks . . . but with exclamation points.

Anonymous

The genius of a good leader is to leave behind him a situation which common sense, without the grace of genius, can deal with successfully.

Walter Lippmann

A constant effort to keep his party together, without sacrificing either principle or the essentials of basic strategy, is the very stuff of political leadership. Macmillan was canonized for that.

Sir Harold Wilson

Whatever the (political) style we choose and whether we rehabilitate words like charisma or hero worship, there is a missing factor in leadership today. . . . The problems that politicians deal with are great; the expectations of their electorates are great; the politicians themselves are not. This is the circular nightmare that the Austrian writer Karl Kraus prophesied as early as the beginning of this century; the importance of the play has increased as the stature of the actors has diminished.

Arianna Stassinopoulos

It has always seemed to me that a sense of history and a rich, abundant and consciously cultivated inner life is an important sustaining element in trying times for people who hold high public office.

Ted Ray

Macmillan, like Churchill, Disraeli, Jefferson, Lincoln, Teddy Roosevelt and others, cultivated an inner life as a support for the critical elements of success in a political leader: administrative ability, oratorical skill, intellectual force, courage, strength of character, hard work and ambition.

Ted Ray

He [David Lloyd George] did not care in which direction the car was traveling, so long as he remained in the driver's seat.

Lord Beaverbrook

Leadership is the art of getting other people to run with your idea as if it were their own.

Harry S. Truman

The great leaders have always stage-managed their effects.

Charles de Gaulle

I have been underestimated for years. I've done very well that way.

Helmut Kohl

LEGISLATION

I never bother with the details. First, I don't know them—I'm not smart enough. Second, if the chairman of a committee has a problem, he'll come in and spell it out for me.

Sam Rayburn

Hell, don't tell me what the bill says. Tell me what it does.

John Nance Garner

One of the great delusions in the world is the hope that the evils in this world are to be cured by legislation.

Thomas B. Reed

The only thing that counts is 218 votes, and nothing else is real. Anything else is talk. You have to be able to pass a bill. It's better to pass a half-good bill than not pass a bill that I am in love with.

Richard Gephardt

If things are going well, religion and legislation are beneficial, if not, they are of no avail.

Solon

The greatest happiness of the greatest number is the foundation of morals and legislation.

Jeremy Bentham

[Legislation is giving] . . . a direction, a form, a technical dress, and a specific sanction, to the general sense of the community.

Edmund Burke

One can always legislate against specific acts of human wickedness; but one can never legislate against the irrational itself.

Morton Irving Seiden

The law of self-preservation is surer policy than any legislation can be.

Ralph Waldo Emerson

Permissive legislation is the characteristic of a free people.

Benjamin Disraeli

Against human nature one cannot legislate. One can only try to educate it, and that is a slow process with only a distant hope of success.

Bernard Berenson

Certain Greek cities, we are told, had a policy that anyone proposing new laws had to do so from a platform in the public market . . . with a rope around his neck. If the law was adopted . . . they removed the rope. If it was rejected . . . they removed the platform.

Jake Garn

LEGISLATORS/LEGISLATURE

So long as the present system of electioneering continues the Legislature must be made up of all kinds of materials.

Massachusetts spy

. . . Hence in Massachusetts the worst men get into the Legislature. Several members of that Body had lately been convicted of infamous crimes. Men of indigence, ignorance and baseness, spare no pains, however dirty, to carry their point against men who are superior to the artifices practised.

Elbridge Gerry
at the Constitutional Convention, 1787

I went to the store the other day to buy a bolt for our front door, for as I told the storekeeper, the Governor was coming here. "Aye," said he, "and the Legislature, too." "Then I will take two bolts," said I. He said that there had been a steady demand for bolts and locks of late, for our protectors were coming.

Henry David Thoreau

One feels, in reading these multiform provisions, as if the legislature was a rabbit seeking to issue from its burrow to ravage the crops wherever it could, and the people of the State were obliged to close every exit because they could not otherwise restrain the inveterate propensity to mischief.

Lord James Bryce

Ignorance, idleness and vice may be sometimes the only ingredient for qualifying a legislator.

Jonathan Swift

[Legislator]. A person who goes to the capital of his country to increase his own.

Ambrose Bierce

No man's life, liberty or property are safe while the legislature is in session.

1 Tucker 245 (N.Y. Surr. 1866)

The legislature is like a cockroach. It's not what they eat and cart away . . . it's what they fall into and mess up.

Anonymous

The legislature is like a septic tank . . . all the big clumps rise to the top.

Martin Hatcher

Legislators are drowning in tax proposals while scrambling to find some miracle life raft to appease government's Moby Dick appetite.

Salem, Oregon, Statesman Journal

It is really more questionable than may be first thought, whether Bonaparte's dumb legislature, which said nothing and did much, may not be preferable to one which talks much and does nothing.

Thomas Jefferson

The great single virtue of a strong legislature is not what it can do but what it can prevent.

J.William Fulbright

I think I can say, and say with pride, that we have some legislatures that bring higher prices than any in the world.

Mark Twain

I needed the good will of the legislature for four states. I "formed" the legislative bodies with my own money. I found that it was cheaper that way.

Jay Gould

Now and then an innocent man is sent to the legislature.

Frank McKinney Hubbard

The speed at which the legislative process seems to work is in inverse proportion to your enthusiasm for the bill.

Pierre DuPont

The length of debate varies inversely with the complexity of the issue. The corollary: "When the issue is simple and everyone understands it, debate is almost interminable."

Robert Knowles

The time spent on any item on an agenda will be in inverse proportion to the sum involved.

C. Northcote Parkinson

The legislature is the only body in which the sum of the parts is greater than the whole.

Paul Schauer

The legislature is a circus that is dominated by its side shows.

Ron Strahle

Legislatures are mostly creatures of the immediate, not the important.

William Hauck

In all legislative assemblies, the greater the number composing them may be, the fewer will be the men who will in fact direct their proceedings.

Alexander Hamilton

Trade and commerce, if they were not made of India rubber, would never manage to bounce over the obstacles which legislators are continually putting in their way.

Henry David Thoreau

Then the Legislature goes and passes a law increasin' the liquor tax or some other tax in New York City, takes half the proceeds for the State Treasury and cuts down the farmers' taxes to suit. It's as easy as rollin' off a log—when you've got a good workin' majority and no conscience to speak of.

George Washington Plunkitt

Never poke fun at legislators . . . or anyone else with the power to route a state highway through your bedroom.

Nosmo King

This legislature is composed of largely intelligent people. Some of them are large. Some of them are intelligent. Some are both. Some are neither.

Jim Lillpop

Nearly every young man who happens to be elected a member of his state legislature is pointed to by his friends and his local newspaper as on his way to the White House.

Calvin Coolidge

I'm inclined to believe that it would be best to choose members of the Legislature quite at random. No matter how stupid they were, they could not be more stupid than the average legislator under the present system. Certainly they'd be measurably more honest, taking one with another. Finally, there would be the advantage that all of them had got their jobs unwillingly, and were eager, not to spin out their sessions endlessly but to get home as soon as possible.

Unidentified quote from Tom Gavin column

LEGISLATORS IN ACTION

Legislators are generally thought of as models of dignity and decorum. Certainly that's the image the senators and representatives wish to project to their constituents and the public-at-large. After all, the making of the public's laws is a serious, solemn business, definitely nothing to joke about.

Again, that's the image. But as anyone knows who has watched a legislative body in action, there's another, more human side. Legislators often find themselves operating in a daffy world of malaprops, misstatements and mixed metaphors where the words don't quite come out as intended.

Let's begin with creatures, both the four-legged and feathered kind. Animals and birds of various kinds have come in for more than their share of verbal legislative abuse. In the interest of avoiding any possible embarrassment, the author has opted not to identify any of the individuals who were responsible for these "words of wisdom":

- We're running sacred cows up the flagpole to see if anyone salutes.

- It's time to grab the bull by the tail and look it in the eye.

- You've got to stop milking that dead horse.

- That's a horse of a different feather.

- Let's not beat a dead horse to death.

- I smell a rat and intend to nip it in the bud.

- A lot of sheep are going to come home to roost.

- If we don't stop shearing the wool off the sheep that lays the golden egg, we'll pump it dry.

Anatomy is another subject that lawmakers have addressed in unusual fashion:

- I realize my face is not a household word in Maryland.

- That argument falls on false ears.

- My colleague is listening with a forked ear.

- If you think those eastern states are going to sit there and take this lying down . . .

- As I was sitting on my thought a seat struck me.

- Jeez, the only time I got to open my mouth was to change feet.

Legislators have had some interesting comments regarding the manner in which they carry out their duty to serve the public:

- There comes a time to put principle aside and do what's right.

- It takes real courage to vote against your convictions.

- Anyone can carry a good bill; it is really hard to get a bad bill passed.

- It's a step in the right direction, it's the answer, and it's constitutional, which is even better.

- To hell with the public! I'm here to represent the people!

Then there are the mixed metaphors: more than one legislator have mixed verbal apples and oranges in unique ways:

- The sword of Damocles is hanging over Pandora's box.

- The ship of state is sailing off its track.

- Now we are changing the tune in the middle of the stream.

- They're hanging by the thread of their bootstrap.

- If it weren't for the Rural Electric Associations, we farmers would still be watching television by candlelight.

- I favor this irrigation bill in order that we may turn the barren hills of my state into fruitful valleys.

- It's time to swallow the bullet.

- At a time when we should be biting bullets, we're here gumming marshmallows.

- If Cal Coolidge were alive today to witness this scene, he'd roll over in his grave.

On more than one occasion, legislators have said things they wish they could take back. Some not so modest examples:

- I defend anyone's right to agree with me.

- He was absolutely right, to a certain extent.

- I will probably definitely go for it.

- These are not my figures I'm quoting. They're the figures of someone who knows what he's talking about.

- I think I know more about this bill than I understand.

- Now we've got them right where they want us.

- Before I give you the benefit of my remarks, I'd like to know what we're talking about.

- Mr. Speaker, what bill did we just pass?

- When I started in talking, I was for the bill; but the longer I talk, the more I know I'm against it.

- I've tried everything else to convince you. Now I'm going to be sensible.

- Remember, if you conquer yourself, you conquer the greatest evil on earth.

- I believe in capital punishment, so long as it ain't too severe.

- I don't see anything wrong with saving human life. That would be good politics, even for us.

- I cannot allow my colleague's ignorance, however vast, to offset my intelligence, however small.

- This bill is a phony with a capital F.

- When we get to that bridge we'll jump.

- You can't see the forest through the trees.

- I've seen the wisdom of my mistake.

- I'm getting paranoid. Even my friends are out to get me.

- Ninety-nine percent of my constituents are 100 percent behind me on this bill.

- I don't think people appreciate how difficult it is to be a pawn of labor.

- We're caught between the dog and the fire hydrant.

- Nothing is too good for the people of Colorado . . . and that's exactly what they're going to get.

- I urge you to pass an anecdote for this crime.

- This amendment is the lesser of two weevils.

- I am diabolically opposed to this.

- This body is becoming entirely too laxative about some matters.

- Mr. Chairman, fellow members and guests, that's a goddamn lie.

- This bill is the worst misjustice of carriage I have ever seen.

- If you can't stand the kitchen, stay out of the heat.

On another occasion a lawmaker was trying to compliment a colleague for the way he chaired the debate on a bill dealing with abortions:

- You've been as neuter as possible on this abortion bill.

Finally, perhaps the all-time classic. The lawmaker who stood at the microphone with a perplexed look and uttered the immortal words:

I misquoted myself.

LIBERALS

A Liberal is a man who uses his legs and his hands at the behest—at the command—of his head.

Franklin D. Roosevelt

A man with both feet planted firmly in the air.

Adlai Stevenson

A man who leaves the room when the fight begins.

Heywood Broun

A liberal is one who loves the world, but hates his neighbors.

Anonymous

A liberal is a person whose interests aren't at stake at the moment.

Willis Player

A liberal is a man too broadminded to take his own side in a quarrel.

Robert Frost

The liberals can understand everything but people who don't understand them.

Lenny Bruce

A liberal is a man who is willing to spend somebody else's money.

Carter Glass

A liberal is a conservative who hasn't been mugged yet.

Frank Rizzo

Liberalism seems to be related to the distance people are from the problem.

Whitney M. Young, Jr.

What the liberal really wants is to bring about change which will not in any way endanger his position.

Stokely Carmichael

It's easier to be a liberal a long way from home.

Don Price

To the modern liberal mind, the word discipline has an almost pornographic sound.

Donald Barr

Though I believe in liberalism, I find it difficult to believe in liberals.

G.K. Chesterton

We who are liberal and progressive know that the poor are our equals in every sense except that of being equal to us.

Lionel Trilling

Liberal institutions straightway cease from being liberal the moment they are soundly established: once this is attained no more grievous and more thorough enemies of freedom exist than liberal institutions.

Nietzsche

It is a Hamlet-like torture to be truly liberal.

Leonard Bernstein

Liberal—a power worshipper without the power.

George Orwell

Liberals! They're not leaders! If they were real leaders they'd understand that their style of politicking and self-aggrandizement is what's destroying the capacity of any of us to get anywhere.

Bella Abzug

If I believe in something, I will fight for it with all I have. But I do not demand all or nothing. I would rather get something than nothing.

Professional liberals want the fiery debate. They glory in defeat. The hardest job for a politician today is to have the courage to be a moderate. It's easy to take an extreme position.

Hubert Humphrey

The liberal . . . is better at inventing reforms than in insuring that they are well and honestly administered.

John Kenneth Galbraith

To be absolutely honest, what I feel really bad about is that I don't feel worse. There's the ineffectual liberal's problem in a nutshell.

Michael Frayn

As the intelligent are liberals, I am on the side of the idiots.

Maurice Baring

They've got a sense of injustice bigger than anyone else, but not so much a sense of justice—that is, they don't want to face the consequences.

Romain Gary

The liberal is accustomed to appearing radical to conservatives, counter-revolutionary to radicals, and as a fink to activists of all persuasions.

Harry S. Ashmore

Compassion is the albatross of the Liberals.

J.B. Priestley

LIES

The first rule of politics is not to lie to somebody unless it is absolutely necessary.

Russell Long

A lie is an abomination unto the Lord, and an ever present help in time of need.

John Tyler Morgan

The political lie has become a way of bureaucratic life. It has been called by the more genteel name of "news management." I say here and now, let's call it what it is: lying.

Walter Cronkite

Every government is run by liars and nothing they say should be believed.

I.F. Stone

Under current law, it is a crime for a private citizen to lie to a government official, but not for the government official to lie to the people.

Donald Fraser

I'm not smart enough to lie.

Ronald Reagan

[Nixon]. He's one of the few in the history of this country to run for high office talking out of both sides of his mouth at the same time and lying out of both sides.

Harry S. Truman

I have never known first-rate politicians to tell a deliberate lie. They colour and exaggerate, but they avoid a lie because of the heavy risk of being tripped up.

David Lloyd George

I do not mind lying, but I hate inaccuracy.

Samuel Butler (novelist)

Half a truth is often a great lie.

Benjamin Franklin

Lying increases the creative faculties, expands the ego, and lessens the frictions of social contacts.

Clare Boothe Luce

A lie consists in not speaking the truth to one who has a right to know it.

Anonymous

If your opponent calls you a liar, call him a thief.

Big Bill Thompson

Liar, n.
A lawyer with a roving commission.

Ambrose Bierce

A lie can travel half way around the world while the truth is putting on its shoes.

Mark Twain

One of the most striking differences between a cat and a lie is that a cat has only nine lives.

Mark Twain

A little inaccuracy saves a world of explanation.

C.E. Ayres

A statesman is an easy man,
He tells his lies by rote;
A journalist makes up his lies
And takes you by the throat;
So stay at home and drink your beer
And let the neighbors vote.

William Butler Yeats

Propaganda is that branch of lying which often deceives your friends without ever deceiving your enemies.

Walter Lippmann

That's not a lie, it's a terminological inexactitude.

Alexander Haig

LOBBYISTS

Corruption has erected her court on the heights of the Hudson, in the avenues of Albany, in the lobby of the legislature. . . . Her throne was the lobby.

Dennis Lynch

They are called by way of honorable distinction Lobby-members because they form a sort of third estate, or legislative chamber in the lobby.

Paulding New Mirror

The lobby are becoming corrupt and impudent.

William Seward

. . . That higher legislative body the lobby.

New York Tribune

The Senator talks of a lobby being here. That is always the cry when anything comes up. "There is a lobby."

Gail Hamilton

Women are said to be the most active and successful lobbyists at Washington.

Lord James Bryce

Women make excellent lobbyists as they are more plausible than men, and cannot be shaken off as rudely.

Edward Winslow Martin

CHUCK HENNING

Washington is honeycombed with lobbyists. The hotels are full of them.
Kenneth B. McKellar

A president only tells congress what they should do. Lobbyists tell 'em what they will do.
Will Rogers

A lobbyist is anyone who opposes legislation I want. A patriot is anyone who supports me.
James A. Reed

Contrary to tradition, against the public morals, and hostile to good government, the lobby has reached such a position of power that it threatens government itself. Its size, its power, its capacity for evil; its greed, trickery, deception and fraud condemn it to the death it deserves.
Hugo Black

Lobbyists are the touts of protected industries.
Winston S. Churchill

What we do is find the Congressman's family doctor and get him to work on the Congressman.
Unidentified AMA official

It's all nonsense, this business of writing to members of the Senate and House asking them to vote for this bill or that. The thing to do is to go after them.
Mark Twain

In Congress, from my experience, the fellow that makes the most noise, and the fellow that makes the most demands, that keeps his problems in front of them all the time, he gets service. If he doesn't; if he depends upon somebody else to do it for him, he is going to get what we all get when we don't go after the thing the way we ought to—nothing.
Joseph Grundy

Lobbyists really are men of revolutionary background—they are careful to see that no one who is taxed is unrepresented.
Eugene McCarthy

If you can't drink their booze, take their money, fool with their women, and then vote against 'em, you don't belong in politics.
Jesse Unruh

If there is a bill in the Legislature makin' it easier for the liquor dealers, I am for it every time.
George Washington Plunkitt

Competent lobbyists can present the most persuasive arguments in support of their positions. Indeed, there is no more effective manner of learning all important arguments and facts on a controversial issue than to have the opposing lobbyists present their case.

John F. Kennedy

The legislators know that the lobbyist is a useful appendage, as important in his own way as the press, and better informed in his own particular field. Many a lobbyist, because of his special knowledge, has saved a legislator from looking foolish.

Warren Moscow

I used to think one plus one equals two. But since I've come to the Legislature, I've learned that one plus one equals one-and-a-half in one man's viewpoint and two-and-a half in another man's viewpoint. I'm suspicious of both sides.

Carl Bledsoe

LOSING CANDIDATES

You may all go to Hell, and I will go to Texas.

Davy Crockett
on being defeated for reelection to Congress

Someone asked me, as I came in, down the street, how I felt, and I was reminded of a story that a fellow townsman of ours used to tell— Abraham Lincoln. They asked him how he felt once after an unsuccessful election. He said he felt like a little boy who stubbed his toe in the dark. He said that he was too old to cry, but it hurt too much to laugh.

Adlai Stevenson
after being defeated in the 1952 presidential election

Disappointed yes; bruised, no.

John Anderson

I am reminded of the drunk who, when he had been thrown down the stairs of a club for the third time, gathered himself up, and said, "I am on to those people. They don't want me in there."

William Jennings Bryan
after third defeat as presidential candidate

Show me a good loser and I'll show you a loser.

Knute Rockne

The voters have spoken—the bastards.

Morris Udall
acknowledging his loss in 1976 presidential primary election

I felt like I had been squashed in a giant compactor.

Kitty Dukakis

M

MAJORITY

The Majority is always in the wrong.

Mark Twain

Hain't we got all the fools in town on our side? And ain't that a big enough majority in any town?

Mark Twain

All politics are based on the indifference of the majority.

James Reston

When you get too big a majority, you're immediately in trouble.

Sam Rayburn

All the wisdom in the world consists in scouting with the majority.

Thomas B. Reed

One, with God, is always a majority, but many a martyr has been burned at the stake while the votes were being counted.

Thomas B. Reed

One with the law is a majority.

Calvin Coolidge

One man with courage makes a majority.

Andrew Jackson

A majority is always the best repartee.

Benjamin Disraeli

The most may err as grossly as the few.

John Dryden

Any man more right than his neighbors constitutes a majority of one.

Henry David Thoreau

I hear many condemn these men because they were so few. When were the good and brave ever in a majority?

Henry David Thoreau

Success, recognition, and conformity are the bywords of the modern world where everyone seems to crave the anesthetizing security of being identified with the majority.

Martin Luther King, Jr.

If by mere force of numbers a majority should deprive a minority of any clearly written constitutional right, it might, in a moral point of view, justify revolution—certainly would if such a right were a vital one.

Abraham Lincoln

All, too, will bear in mind this sacred principle, that though the will of the majority is in all cases to prevail, that will to be rightful must be reasonable; that the minority possess their equal rights, which equal law must protect, and to violate would be oppression.

Thomas Jefferson

The great silent majority.

Richard M. Nixon

Finally, this story about President Abraham Lincoln, which involves a different kind of majority. It's said that during a Cabinet meeting, the president called for a vote on the issue of emancipating the slaves. The Cabinet members all voted "no." Whereupon Mr. Lincoln raised his right hand and said:

The ayes have it.

MEDIA

We are two cocks in dispute over the same dunghill.

Julian Critchley
on the politician and the broadcaster

There's this symbiotic relationship between the press and politicians. It's like the great apes that sit around and pick the fleas off one another.

Richard Lamm

In this cannibalistic society, the media feed off the politicians and the politicians feed off the media. We need each other.

Gene Amole

They can't operate without us and we can't operate without them.

Cokie Roberts

The Politicians View the Press

I am one person who can truthfully say, "I got my job through the *New York Times.*"

John F. Kennedy

A newspaper is the lowest thing there is.

Richard Daley

Accuracy is to a newspaper what virtue is to a lady, except that a newspaper can always print a retraction.

Adlai Stevenson

Newspaper editors are men who separate the wheat from the chaff, and then print the chaff.

Adlai Stevenson

Journalists do not live by words alone, although sometimes they have to eat them.

Adlai Stevenson

While they shriek for "freedom of the press" when there is no slightest threat of that freedom, they deny to citizens that freedom from the press to which the decencies of life entitle them. They misrepresent, they distort, they color, they blackguard, they lie.

Harold Ickes

The newspapers sir, they are the most villainous, licentious, abominable, infernal—Not that I ever read them! No, I make it a rule never to look into a newspaper.

Richard Brinsley Sheridan

"I believe that nothing in the newspapers is ever true," said Madame Phoebus. "And that is why they are so popular," added Euphrosyne. "The taste of the age being so decidedly for fiction."

Benjamin Disraeli

I read the newspaper avidly. It is my one form of continuous fiction.

Aneurin Bevan

The greatest misfortune that ever befell man was the invention of printing.

Benjamin Disraeli

What the proprietorship of these papers is aiming at is power, and power without responsibility, the prerogative of the harlot throughout the ages.

Stanley Baldwin

Media Critics

The average newspaper, especially of the better sort, has the intelligence of a hillbilly evangelist, the courage of a rat, the fairness of a prohibitionist boob-jumper, the information of a high-school janitor, the taste of a designer of celluloid valentines, and the honor of a police-station lawyer.

H.L. Mencken

This is petrified truth.

Mark Twain
on his former avocation

He was as shy as a newspaper when referring to its own merits.

Mark Twain

Only kings, editors and people with tapeworms have the right to use the editorial "we."

Mark Twain

There are honest journalists like there are honest politicians. When bought they stay bought.

Bill Moyers

No normally constituted feller kin read a daily newspaper without congratulatin' himself that he hain't in jail or a candidate for office.

Frank McKinney Hubbard

Reporter, n.
A writer who guesses his way to the truth and dispels it with a tempest of words.

Ambrose Bierce

I await the hour when a journalist can be driven from the press for venal practices, as a minister can be unfrocked, or a lawyer disbarred.

John Haynes Holmes

The volume of political comment substantially exceeds the available truth, so columnists run out of truth, and then must resort to imagination. Washington politicians, after talking things over with each other, relay misinformation to Washington journalists, who, after intramural discussion, print it where it is thoughtfully read by the same politicians, who generally believe it. It is the only successful closed system for the recycling of garbage that has ever been devised.

John K. Galbraith

A political reporter is essentially a fight promoter.

David Broder

Our [the media's] major obligation is not to mistake slogans for solutions.

Edward R. Murrow

Scratch a scribe in this town and you find a campaign manager.

Mary McGrory

If words were invented to conceal thought, newspapers are a great improvement of a bad invention.

Henry David Thoreau

Deep down under his eyes there was a great fever of thought, but he blotted it out by constantly reading newspapers.

Anthony Carson

Editorial writers are people who enter the battlefield after the battle is over and shoot the wounded.

Neil Goldschmidt

I know that every person employed by a newspaper has a radio in his house because he wants his family to get the news accurately.

Fiorello H. La Guardia

I won't say the papers misquote me, but I sometimes wonder where Christianity would be today if some of those reporters had been Matthew, Mark, Luke and John.

Barry Goldwater

The Senator might remember that the evangelists had a more inspiring subject.

Walter Lippmann
responding to above comment by Goldwater

Don't quote what he says. Say what he means.

Goldwater supporter
suggestion to reporters

THE WIT AND WISDOM OF POLITICS

One of the very worst things you can do to a public office holder is quote comments the official made while running for the job.

Al Knight

When you see yourself quoted in print . . . and you're sorry you said it . . . it suddenly becomes a misquotation.

Laurence J. Peter

The only problem I've had [with the press] is when I've said something dumb and they quoted me accurately.

Harold McCormick

Good! Now we shall have news from hell before breakfast.

William Tecumseh Sherman
upon hearing of the death of three reporters by artillery fire

He will print them, without a doubt, for he cares not what he puts into the press.

William Shakespeare

Things evidently base are not only printed, but many things of truth most falsely set forth.

Sir Thomas Browne

The printing press is either the greatest blessing or the greatest curse of modern times, one sometimes forgets which.

Sir James M. Barrie

Newspapers are unable, seemingly, to discriminate between a bicycle accident and the collapse of civilization.

George Bernard Shaw

Journalism consists in saying "Lord Jones Dead" to people who never knew Lord Jones was alive.

G.K. Chesterton

Journalism is popular, but it is popular mainly as fiction. Life is one world, and life seen in the newspapers is another.

G.K. Chesterton

Journalists say a thing that they know isn't true, in the hope that if they keep on saying it long enough it will be true.

Arnold Bennett

The media, a word that has come to mean bad journalism.

Graham Greene

They consume a considerable quantity of our paper manufacture, employ our artisans in printing, and find business for great numbers of indigent persons.

Joseph Addison

Bad manners make a journalist.

Oscar Wilde

In the old days, men had the rack; now they have the press.

Oscar Wilde

The difference between literature and journalism is that journalism is unreadable, and literature is not read.

Oscar Wilde

Freedom of the Press

What is the liberty of the press? Who can give it any definition which would not leave the utmost latitude for evasion?

Alexander Hamilton
The Federalist (No. 84)

The freedom of the press is one of the great bulwarks of liberty, and can never be restrained but by despotic government.

George Mason

A popular Government, without popular information, or the means of acquiring it, is but a Prologue to a Farce or a Tragedy; or, perhaps both.

James Madison

Liberty cannot be preserved without a general knowledge among the people.

John Adams

Freedom to publish means freedom for all and not for some. Freedom to publish is guaranteed by the Constitution, but freedom to continue to prevent others from publishing is not.

Hugo Black

A free press stands as one of the great interpreters between the government and the people. To allow it to be fettered is to be fettered ourselves.

George Sutherland
Grosjean v. American Press Co., 1935

The security of the nation is not at the ramparts alone. Security also lies in the value of our free institutions. A cantankerous press, an obstinate press, a ubiquitous press must be suffered by those in authority in order to preserve the even greater values of freedom of expression and the right of people to know.

Murray I. Gurfein
opinion denying government's request to restrain
New York Times *from publication of Pentagon Papers*

A free press is not a privilege but an organic necessity in a great society. Without criticism and reliable intelligent reporting, the government cannot govern. For there is no adequate way in which it can keep itself informed about what the people of the country are thinking and doing and wanting.

Walter Lippmann

Freedom of the press is reserved for those who own one.

A.J. Liebling

The free press is the mother of all our liberties and of our progress under liberty.

Adlai Stevenson

Let it be impressed upon your minds, let it be instilled into your children, that the liberty of the press is the palladium of all the civil, political, and religious rights of an Englishman.

Junius

Other Pro-Media Comments

A journalist is a grumbler, a censurer, a giver of advice, a regent of sovereigns, a tutor of nations. Four hostile newspapers are more to be feared than a thousand bayonets.

Napoleon Bonaparte

Newspapers are the schoolmasters of the common people.

Henry Ward Beecher

Democracy becomes a government of bullies tempered by editors.

Ralph Waldo Emerson

Show me a reporter with respect for authority and I'll show you a lousy reporter.

Bob Anglin

It is a newspaper's duty to print the news and raise hell.

The Chicago Times

Hot lead can be almost as effective coming from a linotype as from a firearm.

John O'Hara

There is but one way for a newspaper man to look at a politician, and that is down.

Frank H. Simonds

When a reporter sits down at the typewriter, he's nobody's friend.

Theodore H. White

Both Sides of the Issue

I think it is important for our democratic system of government that every medium of communication between the citizens and their government, particularly the president, be kept open as far as possible.

Harry S. Truman

The kind of news conference where reporters can ask any question they can dream up—directly of the President of the United States—illustrates how strong and vital our democracy is. There is no other country in the world where the chief of state submits to such unlimited questioning.

Harry S. Truman

It seems that every man in the White House [has been] tortured and bedeviled by the so-called free press. They were lied about, misrepresented, and actually libeled, and they had to take it and do nothing.

Harry S. Truman

It is, however, an evil for which there is no remedy, our liberty depends on the freedom of the press, and that cannot be limited without being lost.

Thomas Jefferson

Were it left to me to decide whether we should have a government without newspapers, or newspapers without government I should not hesitate a moment to prefer the latter.

Thomas Jefferson

No government ought to be without censors; and where the press is free, none ever will.

Thomas Jefferson

Perhaps an editor might begin a reformation in some way such as this. Divide his paper into four chapters, heading the 1st, Truths. 2nd,

Probabilities. 3rd, Possibilities. 4th, Lies. The first chapter would be very short.

Thomas Jefferson

Advertisements contain the only truths to be relied on in a newspaper.

Thomas Jefferson

When the press is free, and every man able to read, all is safe.

Thomas Jefferson

The only security of all is in a free press.

Thomas Jefferson

It is my belief that robust criticism of government by the press and the consequent skepticism of the press on the part of government are the necessary ingredients of the relationship between the press and the government in a truly free society.

Sam Ervin

In order to enjoy the inestimable benefits that the liberty of the press ensures, it is necessary to submit to the inevitable evils that it creates.

Alexis de Tocqueville

The liberty of the press is a blessing when we are inclined to write against others, and a calamity when we find ourselves overborne by the multitude of our assailants.

Samuel Johnson

When the president and the press lie down together, it's the public that rises up with the fleas.

Hodding Carter III

Some presidents had their own view on the subject:

In the effort of the press to destroy vice it ought not to neglect virtue.

Calvin Coolidge

[Journalists]. They are a sort of assassins who sit with loaded blunderbusses at the corner of streets and fire them off for hire or for sport at any passenger they may select.

John Quincy Adams

The men with the muck-rakes are often indispensable to the well-being of society; but only if they know when to stop raking the muck.

Theodore Roosevelt

I never did believe that newspapermen belonged in politics any more than politicians belonged in the newspaper business.

Harry S. Truman

You know what ought to happen in this country to even things out, reporters ought to have to run for office. Politicians ought to have to write political stories.

Gary Hart

Objectivity
... Objectivity often leans over backward so far that it makes the news business merely a transmission belt for pretentious phonies.

Elmer Davis

If I were objective or if you were objective or if anyone was, he would have to be put away somewhere in an institution because he'd be some sort of vegetable.

David Brinkley

Show me a man who claims he is objective, and I'll show you a man with illusions.

Henry R. Luce

What Is News?
There ain't no news in being good. You might write the doings of all the convents in the world on the back of a postage stamp and have room to spare.

Finley Peter Dunne

Harmony seldom makes a headline.

Silas Bent

Women, wampum and wrongdoing are always news.

Stanley Walker

News is something that someone, somewhere does not want to see in a newspaper.

Robert Emmit Cox

All I have to do to get a story on the front page of every one of the AP's two thousand clients is to mention in the lead a treatment for piles, ulcers or sexual impotence—three conditions that every telegraph editor has, or is worried about.

Alton Blakeslee

Journalism is literature in a hurry.

Matthew Arnold

Literature is the art of writing something that will be read twice; journalism what will be grasped at once.

Cyril Connolly

An editor cannot always act as he would prefer. He is often obliged to bow to the wishes of the public in unimportant matters. Politics are the most important thing in life—for a newspaper.

Henrik Ibsen

What the mass media offer is not popular art, but entertainment which is intended to be consumed like food, forgotten and replaced by a new dish.

W.H. Auden

To a newspaperman a human being is an item with a skin wrapped around it.

Fred Allen

The art of newspapering is to stroke a platitude until it purrs like an epigram.

Don Marquis

The news is twisted by the emphasis on firstness, on the novel and sensational; by the personal interests of the owners; and by the pressure groups.

Report of the Commission on the Freedom of the Press, 1947

Television

This instrument can teach. It can illuminate; yes, it can even inspire. There is a great and perhaps decisive battle to be fought against ignorance, intolerance and indifference.

Edward R. Murrow

Practice whatever the big truth is so that you can say it in forty seconds on camera.

Newt Gingrich

The people who plan campaigns now tell you "whether it's advertising or coverage, don't make a half-hour program or even fifteen minutes." They want those thirty-second bites, or less. It's not so much selling a message. We're just trying to convey an impression.

Russell Long

The impact of immedicacy created by TV has placed a premium not on reflections and reason but on the glib answer and bland statement. The politician is concerned with public relations not with public principles.

Richard B. Morris

I find television very educating. Every time somebody turns on the set I go into the other room and read a book.

Groucho Marx

They call television a medium because it's rare when it's done well.

Fred Allen

Television is to news what bumper strips are to philosophy.

Sign in press room at Colorado State House

Assorted Other Media Observations

The media, far from being a conspiracy to dull the political sense of the people, could be viewed as a conspiracy to disguise the extent of political indifference.

David Riesman

Journalism will kill you, but it will keep you alive while you're at it.

Horace Greeley

Every journalist has a novel in him, which is an excellent place for it.

Russell Lynes

People say they do not believe the newspapers, but they all do believe them. That is the trouble.

Clarence Darrow

There are two forces that carry light to all corners of the globe—the sun in the heavens and the Associated Press down here.

Mark Twain

Newspapermen must organize themselves into a profession . . . a group of men voluntarily under pledge to an idea which supercedes all money considerations.

John Haynes Holmes

A journalist is to a politician as a barking dog is to a chicken thief.

Mike Royko

It's true our credibility was so bad I couldn't believe my own leaks.

Bill Moyers

On Getting Along with the Media

I have noticed that nothing I never said ever did me any harm.

Calvin Coolidge

If it ain't gonna read tomorrow don't do it today.

John Bragg

Never lose your temper with the Press or the public is a major rule of political life.

Christabel Pankhurst

Never argue with a man who buys ink by the barrel.

William Greener

He [President Reagan] has a few weeks to act on Henry Kissinger's principle: Whatever must be revealed eventually should be revealed immediately.

George Will

The public, more often than not, will forgive mistakes, but it will not forgive trying to wriggle and weasel out of one.

Lewis Grizzard

I do offer this general guide to the behavior of voters: the more willing a public person is to talk about his private life, the less the public seems to care.

Jeff Greenfield

I'm not going to say anything terribly important tonight, so you can all put your crayons away.

James Earl Carter, Jr.

We've uncovered some embarrassing ancestors in the not-too-distant past. Some horse thieves and some people killed on Saturday night. One of my relatives was even in the newspaper business.

James Earl Carter, Jr.

For all their quarrels, the politicians and the network people seemed more like colleagues and symbients than opponents. . . . The politicians and the networks need one another, use each other, and are obsessed with each other's businesses. The politicians are media junkies and the network journalists are political junkies. They talk in codes that only fellow insiders—other politicians and their staffs, consultants, and other political reporters—can fully decipher . . . viewers and voters are excluded.

David Broder

How is the world ruled and how do wars start? Diplomats tell lies to journalists and then believe what they read.

Karl Kraus

News and truth are not the same thing and must be clearly distinguished. . . . The function of news is to signalize an event, the function of truth is to bring to light the hidden facts.

Walter Lippmann

The modern world is not given to uncritical admiration. It expects its idols to have feet of clay, and can be reasonably sure that press and camera will report their exact dimensions.

Barbara Ward

We should always tell the press, freely and frankly, anything they could find out in some other way.

Anthony Jay

MEDIOCRITY

Even if he were mediocre, there are a lot of mediocre judges and people and lawyers. They are entitled to a little representation, aren't they, and a little chance?

Roman Hruska

I am one of the great army of mediocrity which constitutes the majority.

Joseph Cannon

The world is a republic of the mediocrities and always was.

Thomas Carlyle

Men have made a virtue of moderation to limit the ambition of the great, and to console people of mediocrity for their want of fortune and of merit.

La Rochefoucauld

Only the mediocre are always at their best.

Jean Giraudoux

Nothing is thoroughly approved but mediocrity. The majority has established this, and it fixes its fangs on whatever gets beyond it either way.

Pascal

Great spirits have always found violent opposition from mediocrities. The latter cannot understand it when a man does not thoughtlessly submit to hereditary prejudices but honestly and courageously uses his intelligence and fulfills the duty to express the results of his thoughts in clear form.

Albert Einstein

There are certain things in which mediocrity is insupportable—poetry, music, painting, public speaking.

La Bruyère

Jealous mediocrity will even wish to bring genius to the scaffold.

Louis de Saint-Just

MIDDLE OF THE ROAD

A middle course is the safest one for you to take.

Ovid

The middle of the road is all of the usable surface. The extremes, right and left, are in the gutters.

Dwight David Eisenhower

I agree with you that in politics the middle way is none at all.

John Adams

[Pitt] tried to find a middle path and he found one which united the worst of both extremes.

Thomas B. Macaulay

Without the political center there is no majority in the democratic system. Anyone who throws away the center sacrifices his capacity to govern.

Willy Brandt

We know what happens to people who stay in the middle of the road. They get run over.

Aneurin Bevan

MILITARY

Why can't we buy just one airplane and have all the pilots take turns?

Calvin Coolidge

Nothing so comforts the military mind as the maxim of a great but dead general.

Barbara Tuchman

There never was a good war or a bad peace.

Benjamin Franklin

However useless a defense contract, however premature its implementation, however extravagant its cost, an argument to proceed is deemed conclusive (by the Pentagon) on one of two grounds: either the Russians are doing it so we must do it to avoid falling behind, or the Russians are not doing it and therefore we must do it to stay ahead.

Pat Schroeder

We would rather die than be humiliated, and we will pluck out the eyes of those who attack the Arab nation.

Saddam Hussein

He [Saddam Hussein] is neither a strategist, nor is he schooled in the operational art, nor is he a tactician, nor is he a general, nor is he a soldier. Other than that, he's a great military man.

Norman Schwarzkopf

MINORITY

A resolute minority has usually prevailed over an easy-going or wobbly majority whose prime purpose was to be left alone.

James Reston

The thing we have to fear in this country, to my way of thinking, is the influence of the organized minorities, because somehow or other the great majority does not seem to organize. They seem to feel that they are going to be effective because of their own strength, but they give no expression of it.

Al Smith

Ten persons who speak make more noise than ten thousand who are silent.

Napoleon Bonaparte

Because half a dozen grasshoppers under a fern make the field ring with their importunate chink . . . do not imagine that those who make the noise are the only inhabitants of the field.

Edmund Burke

No democracy can long survive which does not accept as fundamental to its very existence the recognition of the rights of the minorities.

Franklin D. Roosevelt

If a man is a minority of one, we lock him up.

Oliver Wendell Holmes, Jr.

When you are in a minority, talk; when you are in a majority, vote.

Roger Sherman

Minorities are valuable people, and on the whole those who are opposed to you are more likely to vote than those who support you.

Richard Crossman

MISTAKES

You have to learn from the mistakes of others. You won't live long enough to make them all yourself.

Anonymous

A man should never be ashamed to own he has been in the wrong, which is but saying, in other words, that he is wiser today than he was yesterday.

Alexander Pope

When I make a mistake it's a beaut.

Fiorello H. La Guardia

We make more progress by owning our faults than by always dwelling on our virtues.

Thomas B. Reed

MODERATION

A thing moderately good is not so good as it ought to be. Moderation in temper is always a virtue; but moderation in principle is always a vice.

Thomas Paine

We are now forming a republican government. Real liberty is neither found in despotism or the extremes of democracy, but in moderate governments.

Alexander Hamilton

Extremism in the pursuit of the Presidency is an unpardonable vice. Moderation in the affairs of the nation is the highest virtue.

Lyndon B. Johnson

I love temperate and moderate natures. An immoderate zeal, even for that which is good, though it does not offend, does astonish me, and puts me to study what name to give it.

Michel de Montaigne

MORALITY

It is a moral and political axiom that any dishonorable act, if performed by oneself, is less immoral than if performed by someone else, who would be less well-intentioned in his dishonesty.

J. Christopher Herold

Those who would treat politics and morality apart will never understand the one or the other.

John Morley

What is moral is what you feel good after and what is immoral is what you feel bad after.

Ernest Hemingway

Morality is a private and costly luxury.

Henry Adams

What is morality in any given time or place? It is what the majority then and there happen to like, and immorality is what they dislike.

Alfred North Whitehead

We know no spectacle so ridiculous as the English public in one of its fits of periodical morality . . .

Benjamin Disraeli

Let us give to our republic a fourth power with authority over the youth, the hearts of men, public spirit, habits, and republican morality. Let us establish this Areopagus to watch over the education of the children, to supervise national education, to purify whatever may be corrupt in the republic, to denounce ingratitude, coldness in the country's service, egotism, sloth, idleness, and to pass judgment upon the first signs of corruption and pernicious example.

Simon Bolivar

Where is the man who owes nothing to the land in which he lives? Whatever that land may be, he owes to it the most precious thing possessed by man, the morality of his actions and the love of virtue.

Jean-Jacques Rousseau

In statesmanship get the formalities right, never mind about the moralities.

Mark Twain

The principles of public morality are as definite as those of the morality of private life; but they are not identical.

Lord Acton

MUGWUMPS

A "mugwump" in the modern-day political lexicon is generally thought of as (1) an "unaffiliated" or "independent" voter—one who has declined to register as a member of a political party; or (2) a person who, for one reason or another (often associated with employment), may be active in the functions of both the Republican and Democratic parties but retains the "unaffiliated" status:

I don't belong to either party; I'm a mugwump.

A mugwump is a person educated beyond his intellect.

Horace Porter

A mugwump is one of those boys who always has his mug on one side of the political fence and his wump on the other.

Albert J. Engel

NOMINATIONS

Nominee, n.
A modest gentleman shrinking from the distinction of private life and diligently seeking the honorable obscurity of public office.

Ambrose Bierce

I will not accept if nominated and will not serve if elected.

William Tecumseh Sherman

If nominated I will run to Mexico; if elected I will fight extradition.

Morris Udall
when he was asked in 1980 if he would again consider running for President

If nominated I will not serve and if elected I will not run.

Richard Lamm
when asked if he would run for U.S. Senate

I do not choose to run.

Calvin Coolidge

Whatever I do will depend on whether or not it will help me get the nomination.

George Bush

Talk about presidential timber. Why, man, they had a whole lumber-yard of it here. There were so many being nominated that some of the men making the nomination speeches had never even met the men they were nominating. I know they never had, from the way they talked about them.

Will Rogers

His long speech would have stopped the nomination in a Democratic convention of Thomas Jefferson running on a ticket with Andrew Jackson.

William Allen White

They could look much farther and do much worse and I think they will.

Thomas B. Reed
when asked if he would be nominated for President

OPINIONS

One of the commonest ailments of the present day is premature formation of an opinion.

Frank McKinney Hubbard

The luxury of one's own opinion.

Otto von Bismarck

It is not best we should all think alike; it is difference of opinion which makes horse races.

Mark Twain

Nothing is more conducive to peace of mind than not having any opinion at all.

Georg Christoph Lichtenberg

OPPOSITION

No government can be long secure without a formidable Opposition.

Benjamin Disraeli

The Duty of an Opposition is to Oppose.

Randolph Churchill

When I first came into Parliament, Mr. Tierney, a great Whig authority, used always to say that the duty of an Opposition was very simple—it was to oppose everything and propose nothing.

Lord Stanley

When the Government of the day and the Opposition of the day take the same side, one can almost be sure that some great wrong is at hand.

Anonymous

The delight of political life is altogether in opposition. . . . The very inaccuracy which is permitted to opposition is in itself a charm.

Anthony Trollope

To my mind, the chief objective of an Opposition should be to make the voters feel that the Opposition, in both personnel and ideas, is as different as possible. All Governments in time begin to decay; people begin to feel that a change would do no harm. But they need to see the nature of the change; to find themselves confronted by a choice, a clear choice between differences.

Sir Robert Menzies

Opposition, n.
In politics the party that prevents the Government from running amuck by hamstringing it.

Ambrose Bierce

A good statesman, like any other sensible human being, always learns more from his opponents than from his fervent supporters. For his supporters will push him to disaster unless his opponents show him where the dangers are. So, if he is wise, he will often pray to be delivered from his friends, because they will ruin him. But, though it hurts, he ought also to pray never to be left without opponents; for they keep him on the path of reason and good sense.

Walter Lippmann

I tolerate with the utmost latitude the right of others to differ from me in opinion without imputing to them criminality. I know too well the weakness and uncertainty of human reason to wonder at its different results. Both of our political parties, at least the honest part of them, agree conscientiously in the same object—the public good; but they differ essentially in what they deem the means of promoting that good . . .

. . . Which is right, time and experience will prove. . . . With whichever opinion the body of the nation concurs, that must prevail. My anxieties on this subject will never carry me beyond the use of fair and honorable means, of truth and reason; nor have they ever lessened my esteem for moral worth, nor alienated my affections for a single friend, who did not first withdraw himself from me.

Thomas Jefferson

What country can preserve its liberties, if its rulers are not warned from time to time, that this people preserve the spirit of resistance?

Thomas Jefferson

I respect only those who resist me, but I cannot tolerate them.

Charles de Gaulle

PAPERWORK

It's all papers and forms, the entire Civil Service is like a fortress made of papers, forms and red tape.

Alexander Ostrovsky

Thou hast most traitorously corrupted the youth of the realm in erecting a grammar school; and whereas, before, our forefathers had no other books but the score and the tally, thou hast caused printing to be used; and, contrary to the king, his crown and dignity, thou hast built a paper-mill.

William Shakespeare

Government defines the physical aspects of man by means of the Printed Form, so that for every man in the flesh there is an exactly corresponding man on paper.

Jean Giraudoux

We can lick gravity, but sometimes the paperwork is overwhelming.

Werner von Braun

The more directives you issue to solve a problem the worse it gets.

Jack Robertson

No inanimate thing will move from one place to another without a piece of paper that goes along telling someone where to move it.

Charles E. Wilson

Too often I find that the volume of paper expands to fill the available briefcases.

Jerry Brown

The man whose life is devoted to paperwork has lost the initiative. He is dealing with things that are brought to his notice, having ceased to notice anything for himself. He has been essentially defeated by his job.

E. Northcote Parkinson

PARLIAMENT

England is the Mother of Parliaments.

John Bright

We all know what Parliament is, and we are all ashamed of it.

Robert Louis Stevenson

There is hardly a person in the House of Commons worth painting, though many of them would be better for a little whitewashing.

Oscar Wilde

If a traveler were informed that such a man was leader of the House of Commons he may begin to comprehend how the Egyptians worshipped an insect.

Benjamin Disraeli
on Lord John Russell

For shame, get you gone; give place to honester men; to those who will more faithfully discharge their trust.

Oliver Cromwell
dissolving the rump of the Long Parliament in April 1653

House of Lords—like a glass of champagne that stood for five days.

Clement Attlee

A severe though not unfriendly critic of our institutions said that "the cure for admiring the House of Lords was to go and look at it."

Walter Bagehot

The British House of Lords is the British Outer Mongolia for retired politicians.

Anthony Wedgwood Benn

The House of Lords is a model of how to care for the elderly.

Frank Field

The House of Lords must be the only institution in the world which is kept efficient by the persistent absenteeism of most of its members.

Lord Samuel

If, like me, you are over ninety, frail, on two sticks, half dead and half blind, you stick out like a sore thumb in most places, but not in the House of Lords. Besides, they seem to have a bar and a loo within thirty yards in any direction.

Harold Macmillan

The House of Lords has a value . . . it is good evidence of life after death.

Lord Soper

Thank you for your letter. What harm have I ever done to the Labour Party?

Richard Tawney
declining an appointment to the House of Lords

The House of Commons is not so much a gentleman's club as a boy's boarding school.

Shirley Williams

One does wish that there were a few more women in parliament. Then one could be less conspicuous oneself.

Margaret Thatcher

A parliament is nothing but a big meeting of more or less idle people.

Walter Bagehot

The Commons, faithful to their system, remained in a wise and masterly inactivity.

Sir James Mackintosh

The speaker is their mouth, and trusted by them, and so necessary as the House of Commons cannot sit without him.

Sir Edward Coke

Why Sir, you must provide yourself with a good deal of extraneous matter, which you are to produce occasionally, so as to fill up the time; for you must consider, that they do not listen much. If you begin with the strength of your cause, it may be lost before they begin to listen.

Samuel Johnson
advising his biographer, James Boswell, on addressing Commons

A freshman Member of Commons once asked the vaunted Disraeli if the old members were wondering why the newcomer did not speak in the House. Disraeli responded:

Young man, it is better to have them wondering why you do not speak, than wondering why you do.

THE WIT AND WISDOM OF POLITICS

A sophistical rhetorician, inebriated with the exuberance of his own verbosity, and gifted with an egotistical imagination that can at all times command an interminable and inconsistent series of arguments to malign an opponent and to glorify himself.

Benjamin Disraeli
on his nemesis, William E. Gladstone

He speaks to me as if I was a public gathering.

Queen Victoria
on William E. Gladstone

Timidity was fortified with pride, and even the success of my pen discouraged the trial of my voice.

Edward Gibbon
on his silence in Parliament

He is one of those orators of whom it was well said: "Before they get up they do not know what they are going to say; when they are speaking, they do not know what they are saying, and when they sit down, they do not know what they have said."

Winston S. Churchill
on the oratorical talents of Lord Charles Beresford

In his younger days, Churchill once distributed printed copies of his recent speeches to his fellow members. One Liberal Party member acknowledged the gift in the following manner:

Dear Mr. Churchill. Thanks for the copy of your speeches lately delivered in the House of Commons. To quote the late Lord Beaconsfield: "I shall lose no time in reading them."

The first duty, if not the whole duty, of a private member of the House of Commons is to speak as little and to vote as often as he can.

Herbert Asquith

The perfection of Parliamentary style is to utter cruel platitudes with a grave and informing air; and, if a little pomposity be superadded, the House will instinctively recognize the speaker as a Statesman.

George William Russell

Don't lecture them. Don't joke. Don't try and be an orator. Don't be sarcastic. Just talk naturally. . . . One thing the House will NEVER forgive and that is if a Minister misleads it. If you find you have given an answer that isn't true, acknowledge it at once and express your regret. The blame is always on you and not on the Civil Service.

Stanley Baldwin
advice to Sir John Reith on entering Commons

The ability to parry words is highly valued in Parliament: the knack of turning a phrase humorously in order to repel an opponent's verbal attack and turn it to your own advantage. Perhaps the most famous illustration of this occurred in Commons when the Earl of Sandwich predicted John Wilkes would die, either upon the gallows or of some venereal disease. Wilkes' lightning-quick response has become legendary:

That depends, my lord, on whether I embrace your principles or your mistress.

I remember when I was a child being taken to the celebrated Barnum's Circus . . . the exhibit which I most desired to see was the one described as "the Boneless Wonder." My parents judged that the spectacle would be too revolting for my youthful eyes, and I have waited fifty years to see the Boneless Wonder sitting on the Treasury Bench.

Winston S. Churchill
on Ramsey MacDonald

The right honorable gentleman is indebted to his memory for his jests and to his imagination for his facts.

Richard Brinsley Sheridan
on his opponent, Robert Dundas

In one sense the House of Commons is the most unrepresentative of assemblies. It is an elaborate conspiracy to prevent the real clash of opinion which exists outside from finding an appropriate echo within its walls. It is a social shock absorber placed between privilege and the pressure of popular discontent.

Aneurin Bevan

No man is regular in his attendance at the House of Commons until he is married.

Benjamin Disraeli

The British, being brought up on team games, enter their House of Commons in the spirit of those who would rather be doing something else. If they cannot be playing golf or tennis, they can at least pretend that politics is a game with very similar rules.

C. Northcote Parkinson

PARTIES

Those who think that all virtue is to be found in their own party principles push matters to extremes; they do not consider that disproportion destroys a state.

Aristotle

There are men who desire power simply for the sake of the happiness it will bring; these belong chiefly to political parties.

Nietzsche

One step forward, two steps back. ... It happens in the lives of individuals, and it happens in the history of nations and in the development of parties.

V.I. Lenin

We abhor political parties. We are against political parties, and we have none.

Francisco Franco

For me party discipline is a sacred matter, not just lust for power as some people claim: I was brought up that way all my life.

Golda Meir

Party loyalty lowers the greatest men to the petty level of the masses.

La Bruyère

The British

The best Party is but a kind of Conspiracy against the rest of the Nation.

George Savile

All political parties die at last of swallowing their own lies.

John Arbuthnot

The conduct of a losing party never appears right: at least it never can possess the most infallible criterion of wisdom to vulgar judgment—success.

Edmund Burke

A nation without parties is soon a nation without curiosity.

Horace Walpole

Party divisions, whether on the whole operating for good or evil, are things inseparable from free government.

Edmund Burke

A party of order or stability, and a party of progress or reform, are both necessary elements of a healthy state of political life.

John Stuart Mill

He that aspires to be the head of a party will find it more difficult to please his friends than to perplex his foes.

Charles Caleb Colton

The only difference, after all their rout,
Is, that one is in, the other out.

Charles Churchill

It is not becoming to any minister to decry party who has risen by party.
We should always remember that if we were not partisans we should
not be ministers.

Benjamin Disraeli

Damn your principles! Stick to your party.

Benjamin Disraeli

There is no act of treachery or meanness of which a political party is not
capable; for in politics there is no honor.

Benjamin Disraeli

The Conservatives frighten me, the Labour Party terrifies me and the
Liberal Democrats make me suicidal.

A voter speaking to John Major

I always voted at my party's call, and I never thought of thinking for
myself at all.

W.S. Gilbert

The first advice I have to give the party is that it should clean its slate.

Lord Rosebery

It is an error to believe that the world began when any particular party
or statesmen got into office. It has all been going on quite a long time.

Winston S. Churchill

[A] successful Party of the Right must continue to recruit from the
center and even from the left center. Once it begins to shrink into itself
like a snail, it will be doomed.

Harold Macmillan

The Americans

Under democracy one party always devotes its chief energies to trying
to prove that the other party is unfit to rule—and both commonly
succeed, and are right.

H.L. Mencken

The amount of effort put into a campaign by a worker expands in
proportion to the personal benefits that he will derive from his party's victory.

Milton Rakove

Any party which takes credit for the rain must not be surprised if its opponents blame it for the drought.

Dwight Morrow

Man resolves himself into a couple of petrified parties whose adherents learn to vote for their party candidate irrespective of their character.

Mark Twain

Men think they think upon great politicial questions, and they do; but they think with their party, not independently; they read its literature, but not that of the other side; they arrive at convictions, but they are drawn from a partial view of the matter in hand and are of no particular value. They swarm with their party, they feel with their party, they are happy in their party's approval; and where the party leads they will follow, whether for right and honor, or through blood and dirt and a mush of mutilated morals.

Mark Twain

No party is as bad as its leaders.

Will Rogers

There is a hundred things to single you out for promotion in party politics besides ability.

Will Rogers

Ignorance leads Men into a Party, and Shame keeps them from getting out again.

Benjamin Franklin

Let me now ... warn you in the most solemn manner against the baneful effects of the spirit of party.

George Washington

The spirit of party serves always to distract public councils, and enfeeble the public administration.

George Washington

There is nothing I dread so much as the division of the Republic into two great parties, each under its leader. . . . This, in my humble opinion, is to be feared as the greatest political evil under our Constitution.

John Adams

If I could not go to Heaven but with a party I would not go there at all.

Thomas Jefferson

No free country has ever been without parties, which are a natural offspring of Freedom.

James Madison

The public good is disregarded in the conflicts of rival parties.
James Madison

If parties in a republic are necessary to secure a degree of vigilance sufficient to keep the public functionaries within the bounds of law and duty, at that point their usefulness ends.
William Henry Harrison

He serves his party best who serves the country best.
Rutherford B. Hayes

Party honesty is party expedience.
Grover Cleveland

Our government is a government of political parties under the guiding influence of public opinion. There does not seem to be any other method by which a representative government can function.
Calvin Coolidge

The very basis of representative government is a two-party system. It is one of the essential checks and balances against inefficiency, dishonesty, and tyranny.
Herbert Hoover

The American people are quite competent to judge a political party that works both sides of the street.
Franklin D. Roosevelt

Let us not seek the Republican answer or the Democratic answer, but the right answer. Let us not seek to fix the blame for the past. Let us accept our own responsibility for the future.
John F. Kennedy

I think it's very important that we have a two party system. I am a fellow that likes small parties, and the Republican Party is about the size I like.
Lyndon B. Johnson

Political parties serve to keep each other in check, one keenly watching the other.
Henry Clay

The best system is to have one party govern and the other party watch.
Thomas B. Reed

A political party is not made to order. It is the slow development of powerful forces working in our social life. Sound ideas seize upon the human mind.

THE WIT AND WISDOM OF POLITICS

Opinions ripen into fixed convictions. Masses of men are drawn together by common belief and organized about clearly defined principles.

Robert M. La Follette

A party can live only by growing, intolerance of ideas brings its death. ... An organization that depends upon reproduction only for its vote, son taking the place of father, is not a political party, but a Chinese tong; not citizens brought together by thought and conscience, but an Indian tribe held together by blood and prejudice.

Albert Beveridge

Even more important than winning the election is governing the nation. That is the best of a political party—the acid, final test.

Adlai Stevenson

The party permits ordinary people to get ahead. Without the party, I couldn't be a mayor.

Richard Daley

First, this great and glorious country was built up by political parties; second, parties can't hold together if their workers won't get the offices when they win; third, if the parties go to pieces the government they built up must go to pieces, too; fourth, then there'll be h— to pay.

George Washington Plunkitt

All political ideas cannot and should not be channelled into the programs of our two major parties. History has amply proved the virtue of political activity by minority, dissident groups, who innumerable times have been in the vanguard of democratic thought and whose programs were ultimately accepted.

Earl Warren

A sect or party is an elegant incognito devised to save a man from the vexation of thinking.

Ralph Waldo Emerson

The two parties which divide the state, the party of conservatives and the party of innovators, are very old, and have disputed the possession of the world ever since it was made.

Ralph Waldo Emerson

Parties can no more be held together and made to function without organization than any great business can be run without organization. Without organization there would be no parties. Without parties there would be no government.

Frank R. Kent

The disagreement among American political parties, with only a few exceptions, has been over the practical question of how to secure the agreed objective, while conciliating different interests, rather than over ultimate values or over what interest is paramount.

Daniel Boorstin

You cannot influence a Political Party to do right, if you stick to it when it does wrong.

John Bengough

I am neither a Democrat nor a Republican. I'm a registered Whig.

Jack Benny

When you have lived longer in this world and outlived the enthusiastic and pleasing illusions of youth, you will find your love and pity for the race increased tenfold, your admiration and attachment to any particular party or opinion fall away together...this is the most important lesson that a man can learn, that opinions are nothing but the mere result of chance and temperament; that no party is on the whole better than another.

Stanley Baldwin

PARTISANSHIP

Partisanship is our great curse. We too readily assume that everything has two sides and that it is our duty to be on one side or the other.

James Harvey Robinson

A partisanship is what someone else does. When I do it, it is taking a stand.

Roger L. Shinn

PATRIOTISM

Patriotism is a praiseworthy competition with one's ancestors.

Tacitus

No one loves his country for its size or eminence, but because it is his own.

Seneca

Patriotism is a kind of religion; it is the egg from which wars are hatched.

Guy de Maupassant

Patriotism is the passion of fools and the most foolish of passions.

Arthur Schopenhauer

Patriotism is the last refuge of a scoundrel.

Samuel Johnson

A patriot is a fool in ev'ry age.

Alexander Pope

"My country right or wrong" is a thing that no patriot would think of saying except in a desperate case. It is like saying "My mother, drunk or sober."

G.K. Chesterton

Though I love my country, I do not love my countrymen.

Lord Byron

Patriotism is the virtue of the vicious.

Oscar Wilde

Patriotism is the willingness to kill and be killed for trivial reasons.

Bertrand Russell

Patriotism has become a mere national assertion, a sentimentality of flag-cheering with no constructive duties.

H.G. Wells

Patriotism is your conviction that this country is superior to all other countries because you were born in it.

George Bernard Shaw

You'll never have a quiet world till you knock the patriotism out of the human race.

George Bernard Shaw

Patriotism is in political life what faith is in religion.

Lord Acton

Love makes fools, marriage cuckolds, and patriotism malevolent imbeciles.

Paul Leautaud

A politician will do anything to keep his job—even become a patriot.
William Randolph Hearst

When a whole nation is roaring Patriotism at the top of its voice, I am fain to explore the cleanness of its hands and purity of its heart.
Ralph Waldo Emerson

Priests are no more necessary to religion than politicians to patriotism.
John Haynes Holmes

No other factor in history, not even religion, has produced so many wars as has the clash of national egotisms sanctified by the name of patriotism.
Preserved Smith

To strike freedom of the mind with the fist of patriotism is an old and ugly subtlety.
Adlai Stevenson

Talking of patriotism, what humbug it is; it is a word which always commemorates a robbery. There isn't a foot of land in the world which doesn't represent the ousting and re-ousting of a long line of successive owners.
Mark Twain

Patriotism is often an arbitrary veneration of real estate above principles.
George Jean Nathan

Patriotism is easy to understand in America; it means looking out for yourself by looking out for your country.
Calvin Coolidge

You're not supposed to be so blind with patriotism that you can't face reality. Wrong is wrong no matter who does it or says it.
Malcolm X

Patriotism in the female sex is the most disinterested of all virtues. Excluded from honors and from offices, we cannot attach ourselves to the State or Government from having held a place of eminence. Even in the freest of countries our property is subject to the control and disposal of our partners, to whom the laws have given a sovereign authority. Deprived of a voice in legislation, obliged to submit to those laws which are imposed on us, is it not sufficient to make us indifferent to the public welfare? Yet all history and every age exhibit instances of patriotic virtue in the female sex; which considering our situation equals the most heroic of yours.
Abigail Adams

PEACE

What we dignify with the name of peace is really only a short truce, in accordance with which the weaker party renounces his claims, whether just or unjust, until such time as he can find an opportunity of asserting them with the sword.

Vauvenargues

Making peace is harder than making war.

Adlai Stevenson

We Smiths want peace so bad we're prepared to kill every one of the Joneses to get it.

I.F. Stone

The peace dividend is peace.

Dan Quayle

The Cold War is now behind us. Let us not wrangle over who won it.
Mikhail Gorbachev

I have three children at home and I want to leave for them a world free of nuclear war. This would be the greatest gift all politicians could give to the children of the world.

Brian Mulroney

PEOPLE

The people will stand for anything. What they can't stand for, they'll fall for.

Ross Winne

The great enemy of reason, virtue, and religion, the Multitude, that numerous piece of monstrosity.

Sir Thomas Browne

The inertia, the indifference, the insubordination and instinctive hostility of the mass of mankind.

H.G. Wells

The giving of love is an education in itself.
Anna Eleanor Roosevelt

A man's home may seem to be his castle on the outside; inside it is more often the nursery.

Clare Boothe Luce

People are usually more convinced by reasons they have discovered themselves than by those found in others.

Pascal

PHILOSOPHERS

There is nothing so absurd but some philosopher has said it.

Cicero

A blind man in a dark room looking for a black cat which isn't there.

Lord Bowen

It's only possible to live happily ever after on a day to day basis.

Margaret Bonanno

I have a simple philosophy. Fill what's empty. Empty what's full. Scratch where it itches.

Alice Roosevelt Longworth

I have a new philosophy. I'm only going to dread one day at a time.

Charles Schulz

A philosophy is characterized more by the formulation of its problems than by its solution of them.

Susanne K. Langer

When you have a philosophy, when you have a set of principles by which you live and upon which you can depend and which the party can run with, when you have principles you don't have to have consultants, you don't have to have big meetings to tell you what it is that needs doing.

William Vander Zalm

PLAGIARISM

When a thing has been said and well said, have no scruple; take it and copy it. Give references? Why should you? Either your readers know where you have taken the passage and the precaution is needless, or they do not know and you humiliate them.

Anatole France

Amongst so many borrowed things, I am glad if I can steal one, disguising and altering it for some new service.

Michel de Montaigne

Immature artists imitate. Mature artists steal.

Lionel Trilling

They lard their lean books with the fat of others' works.

Robert Burton

Great literature must spring from an upheaval in the author's soul. If that upheaval is not present, then it must come from the works of any other author which happen to be handy and easily adapted.

Robert Benchley

Adam was the only man who, when he said a good thing, knew that nobody had said it before him.

Mark Twain

About the most originality that any writer can hope to achieve is to steal with good judgment.

Josh Billings

What is originality? Undetected plagiarism.

William R. Inge

Imitation is the sincerest form of plagiarism.

B.C. comic strip

Whatever has been well said by anyone is mine.

Seneca

PLANNING

Never take anything for granted.

Benjamin Disraeli

No amount of advance planning can take the place of dumb luck.

Anonymous

It's a bad plan that can't be changed.

Publilius Syrus

It is better to have a bad plan than to have no plan at all.

Charles de Gaulle

Let your advance worrying become advanced thinking and planning.

Winston S. Churchill

Our plans miscarry because they have no aim. When a man does not know what harbor he is making for, no wind is the right wind.

Seneca

Make no little plans; for they have no magic to stir men's blood.

Daniel Burnham

I was a great admirer of old D.H. Burnham of Chicago who organized the Chicago regional planning, and he had a motto over his mantel on which was written "MAKE NO LITTLE PLANS." You can always amend a big plan, but you never can expand a little one. I don't believe in little plans. I believe in plans big enough to meet a situation which we can't possibly foresee now.

Harry S. Truman

The finest plans have always been spoiled by the littleness of them that should carry them out. Even emperors can't do it all by themselves.

Bertolt Brecht

I have never yet seen any plan which has not been or ended by the observations of those who were much inferior in understanding to the person who took the lead in the business.

Edmund Burke

I arise in the morning torn between a desire to improve (or save) the world and a desire to enjoy (or savor) the world. This makes it hard to plan the day.

E.B. White

Our actions or policies in foreign affairs seem to be improvised on the spur of the moment. We play by ear without the slightest regard for the harmony of the composition.

J. William Fulbright

PLATFORMS

We are in favor of a law which absolutely prohibits the sale of liquor on Sunday—but we are against its enforcement.

New York Democratic Party platform

A platform is not something you stand on, but something you run on.

Anonymous

A platform is what you start by running on and end by running from.

Anonymous

Platform—something you need to catch a train. After you've caught the train, who needs it?

Anonymous

A political platform is like the platform of a trolley car—not meant to stand on but just to get in on.

Anonymous

A political platform must be built ingeniously so that a candidate can keep standing on it while the opposition is dismantling it plank by plank.

Anonymous

A declaration of unattainable objectives, so phrased and arranged as to arouse the maximum confusion with the minimum sincerity.

Anonymous

Political platforms are for one party to stand on, and the other to jump on.
Arnold H. Glasgow

His political platforms were only wings of a windmill.
Sinclair Lewis

To me, party platforms are contracts with the people.
Harry S. Truman

I have read their platform, and though I think there are some unsound places in it, I can stand upon it pretty well. But I see nothing in it both new and valuable. "What is valuable is not new, and what is new is not valuable."

Daniel Webster

... You know the platform will always be the same—promise everything, deliver nothing.

Will Rogers

I once tabulated the platform pledges of the three national parties over the past ten election campaigns. The promises they made were remarkably similar, varying only in their degree of distributing largess with the taxpayers' dollars: the Tories promised handouts to voters from birth to death; the Liberals from womb to tomb; the Socialists from erection to resurrection.

Peter Newman

POLICY

Policy, like babies, used to be made casually, in response to immediate urges or needs. Now, everything from families to foreign policy, is planned.

Lord Trevelyan

Making policy means making decisions.
Harry S. Truman

My policy is to have no policy.

Abraham Lincoln

This strategy represents our policy for all time. Unless it's changed.

Marlin Fitzwater

POLITICIANS
Nobody has ever said anything on behalf of the politician half so sharp and true as many intelligent men have said against him.

Ferdinand Lundberg

The politician, indeed, like the prostitute, is universally condemned even as he is freely resorted to.

Ferdinand Lundberg

The Greeks
[Politician]. A man of loose tongue, intemperate, trusting to tumult, leading the populace to mischief with empty words.

Euripides

You have all the characteristics of a popular politician: a horrible voice, bad breeding, and a vulgar manner.

Aristophanes

Under every stone lurks a politician.

Aristophanes

It is evident that the state is a creation of nature, and that man is by nature a political animal. And why man is a political animal in a greater measure than any bee or gregarious animal, is clear. For nature does nothing without purpose, and man alone of the animals possesses speech.

Aristotle

Other Nationalities
The politician is an acrobat. He keeps his balance by saying the opposite of what he does.

Maurice Barres

An important art of politicians is to find new names for institutions which under old names have become odious to the public.

Charles-Maurice de Talleyrand-Périgord

Since a politician never believes what he says, he is always astonished when others do.

Charles de Gaulle

In order to become the master, the politician poses as a servant.

Charles de Gaulle

I have come to the conclusion that politics are too serious a matter to be left to the politicians.

Charles de Gaulle

Political leaders rarely originate ideas. Their genius lies in selection and application from the community's stock of remedies.

Arthur M. Schlesinger, Jr.

To be a politician is but to feign ignorance of what you know well, pretend knowledge of what you are totally ignorant, decline to listen to what you hear, attempt what is beyond your capacity, hide what ought to be exposed, appear profound when you are dull-witted and to justify ignoble means by claiming admirable ends.

Pierre de Beaumarchais

Politicians are the same all over. They promise to build a bridge even where there is no river.

Nikita Khrushchev

It is inexcusable for scientists to torture animals; let them make their experiments on journalists and politicians.

Henrik Ibsen

We progress at night while the politicians sleep.

Rio de Janeiro proverb

There's something about politicians, about becoming a politician and being a politician that is so unpalatable that most of the best people in the community won't take it on.

James McLelland

My chief advantage as a politician was that I did not give a damn.

Stanley Melbourne Bruce

The British

. . . A politician . . . one that would circumvent God.

William Shakespeare

Among politicians, the esteem of religion is profitable, the principles of it are troublesome.

Benjamin Whichcote

No man can be a politician, except that he be first a historian or a traveller; for except that he can see what must be, or what may be, he is no politician.

James Harrington

The politician who didn't make mistakes is never a politician, and the politician who admitted them to you wouldn't be a politician.

John Major

What Politician yet e'er scap't his Fate,
Who saving his own Neck not sav'd the State?

John Dryden

Be silent as a politician, for talking may beget suspicion.

Jonathan Swift

It is easier for a camel to go through the eye of a needle, or for a rich man to enter the kingdom of heaven, than for a politician to lay aside disguise.

James Caulfield

He knows nothing; and he thinks he knows everything. That points clearly to a political career.

George Bernard Shaw

Politicians. Little Tin Gods on Wheels.

Rudyard Kipling

The double pleasure of pulling down an opponent, and of raising oneself, is the charm of a politician's life.

Anthony Trollope

Every politician is emphatically a promising politician.

G.K. Chesterton

There's just one rule for politicians all over the world: Don't say in Power what you say in Opposition; if you do, you have to carry out what the other fellows have found impossible.

John Galsworthy

The greatest asset a politician can have is a blameless record as far as women are concerned.

W. Somerset Maugham

THE WIT AND WISDOM OF POLITICS

A politician need never apologize for opportunism in action, but he should always be ashamed of compromise in thought.

Walter Bagehot

Here richly, with ridiculous display,
The politician's corpse was laid away.
While all of his acquaintance sneered and slanged,
I wept; for I had longed to see him hanged.

Hilaire Belloc

Any politician who wishes to be remembered must create a legend about himself; the choice lies between being legendary or being forgotten.

Charles Whibley

No politician has ever yet been able to rule his country, nor has any country ever yet been able to face the world, upon the principles of the Sermon on the Mount.

Frederick Scott Oliver

In taking stock of a politician the first question is not whether he was a good man who used righteous means, but whether he was successful in gaining power, in keeping it, and in governing; whether, in short, he was skillful at his particular craft or a bungler.

Frederick Scott Oliver

Render any politician down and there's enough fat to fry an egg.

Spike Milligan

The proper memory for a politician is one that knows when to remember and when to forget.

John Morley

Timid and interested politicians think much more about the security of their seats than about the security of their country.

Thomas B. Macaulay

It is the business of the speculative philosopher to mark the proper ends of government. It is the business of the politician, who is the philosopher in action, to find out proper means toward those ends, and to employ them with effect.

Edmund Burke

It's the ability to foretell what will happen tomorrow, next month and next year—and to explain afterwards why it did not happen.

Winston S. Churchill
on the essential qualifications for a politician

Politicians make one fundamental mistake when they have been in office. They think that the people who are in office, or who have been in office, are absolutely essential to the government of the country and that no one else is in the least able to carry on affairs. Well, we are a people of 45,000,000 and really, if we cannot produce at least two or three alternative Cabinets, we must be what Carlyle once called us—"a nation of fools."

David Lloyd George

To identify the problems of contemporary society, to locate the men and women who are working for a solution, to evolve policies from ideas, to organize mass movements to campaign for these policies, to convince the people to accept them, to carry through the programme by consent, lubricating the process with wise compromises without losing sight of the objective as he goes along—these are the tasks of the politician.

Anthony Wedgwood Benn

There is no politician who is not ambitious; it is the definition of the animal.

Enoch Powell

Politicians are ambitious not to make important decisions but to say important things.

Richard Crossman

Politicians who have not had time to become acquainted with human nature, are peculiarly ignorant of the desires that move ordinary men and women. Any political party whose leaders knew a little psychology could sweep the country.

Bertrand Russell

Exhortation of other people to do something is the last resort of politicians who are at a loss to know what to do themselves.

Sir Paul Chambers

Politicians can forgive about anything in the way of abuse; they can forgive subversion, revolution, being contradicted, exposed as liars, even ridiculed, but they can never forgive being ignored.

Auberon Waugh

It is a pity, as my husband says, that most politicians are not bastards by birth instead of vocation.

Katharine Whitehorn

In political discussion heat is in inverse proportion to knowledge.

J.G.C. Minchin

A politician rises on the backs of his friends . . . but it is through his enemies he will have to govern afterwards.

Richard Hughes

The Politicians

A politician who steals is worse than a thief. He is a fool. With the grand opportunities all around for a man with political pull, there's no excuse for stealin' a cent.

George Washington Plunkitt

The politicians who make a lastin' success in politics are the men who are always loyal to their friends, even up to the gate of the State prison, if necessary.

George Washington Plunkitt

Politicians are seldom in the right frame of mind for effective work because they are continually guarding their popularity. Roosevelt started getting elected in 1936 before he was even inaugurated in 1932.

Joseph Ely

Politicians give false emphasis to the importance of their work. They read all the political news and suppose everyone else does also.

Joseph Ely

The politician is an educator, and his first responsibility is to educate the people, and one of the techniques of education is to tickle their fancy and their sense of humor.

Adlai Stevenson

A politician can do anything as long as he manipulates the right symbols.

Jerry Brown

Some politicians are dull, but it's in their genes. They would be dull if they were waiters or insurance salesmen or in other jobs of equal stature to politicians.

Willie Brown

The mark of a good politician is the ability to stop at two drinks.

Charles Colson

The politician adjusts manually instead of ideologically. He does something and sees who hollers and then invents a remedy and sees who hollers over the remedy.

T.V. Smith

The typical political leader of the contemporary managerial society is a man of strong will, a high capacity to get himself elected, but no very great conception of what he is going to do when he gets into office.

Henry Kissinger

Bad politicians are sent to Washington by good people who don't vote.

William Simon

Good politicians don't make wrong moves. Doing nothing is sometimes better.

Unidentified Senate aide

A politician's willingness to listen to advice rises in inverse proportion to how badly he thinks he is doing.

Pat Caddell

The politicians were talking themselves red, white and blue in the face.

Clare Boothe Luce

Sooner or later all politicians die of swallowing their own lies.

Clare Boothe Luce

The mistake a lot of politicians make is in forgetting they've been appointed and thinking they've been anointed.

Mrs. Claude Pepper

Your politicians will always be there when they need you.

Jimmy Carter T-shirt, during 1980 election

It's a big mistake to believe that politicians can exist only upon the sound of their titles, as it is to believe that newlyweds can live solely upon love.

James J. Walker

Keep your eyes on the prize.

Jesse Jackson

A politician knows that the best way to be a winner is to make the other side feel it does not have to be a loser.

Thomas B. Reed

The Presidents

Mothers all want their sons to grow up to be President, but they didn't want them to become politicians in the process.

John F. Kennedy

Being a politician is a poor profession. Being a public servant is a noble one.

Herbert Hoover

There are three things worth being—a preacher, a teacher or a politician.

Lyndon B. Johnson

The most successful politician is he who says what everybody is thinking most often and in the loudest voice.

Theodore Roosevelt

Practical politics must not be construed to mean dirty politics . . . The most practical of all politicians is the politician who is clean and decent and upright.

Theodore Roosevelt

A politician knows that his friends are not always his allies, and that his adversaries are not his enemies.

Richard M. Nixon

A politician knows that the best way to be a winner is to make the other side feel it does not have to be a loser. And a politician . . . knows both the name of the game and the rules of the game, and he seeks his ends through the time-honored democratic means.

Richard M. Nixon

I'll speak for the man, or against him, whichever will do him most good.

Richard M. Nixon

I have often said that the one thing worse for a politician than being wrong is being dull. But it is better to be dull than to be silly.

Richard M. Nixon

I've often wondered how some people in positions of this kind . . . manage without having had any acting experience.

Ronald Reagan

The Humorists

I am not a politician, and my other habits are good.

Artemus Ward

I remain just one thing, and one thing only — and that is a clown. It places me on a far higher plane than any politician.

Charles Chaplin

A politician is like quicksilver: if you try to put your finger on him, you will find nothing under it.

Austin O'Malley

The trouble with this country is that there are too many politicians who believe, with a conviction based on experience, that you can fool all of the people all of the time

Franklin P. Adams

I once said cynically of a politician: "He'll double-cross that bridge when he comes to it."

Oscar Levant

You politicians have got to look further ahead; you always got a putter in your hands, when you ought to have a Driver.

Will Rogers

If experience teaches us anything at all, it teaches us this: that a good politician, under democracy, is quite as unthinkable as an honest burglar.

H.L. Mencken

If a politician found he had cannibals among his constituents, he would promise them missionaries for their Sunday dinner.

H.L. Mencken

I'm a terrible softie on most politicians, and I'm terribly fond of them. They're among the few people in America who still work, live by their wits, have no job security, endure brutal hours, and show great ingenuity even when they're thieves. They're the last people who go over Niagara Falls in a barrel—they take risks. Most of them have sufficient ambition to be extremely interesting; an evening spent with a politician is more entertaining than with just about anybody else.

Russell Baker

The Journalists and Other Writers

The professional politician is one of the mysteries of American life, a bundle of paradoxes, shrewd as a fox, naive as a schoolboy. He has a great respect for the people yet treats them like boobs, and is constitutionally unable to keep his mouth shut.

James Reston

All politicians should have three hats—one to throw into the ring, one to talk through, and one to pull rabbits out of if elected.

Carl Sandburg

Successful democratic politicians are insecure and intimidated men. They advance politically only as they placate, appease, bribe, seduce, bamboozle or otherwise manage to manipulate the demanding and threatening elements in their constituencies.

Walter Lippmann

Politicians tend to live "in character," and many a public figure has come to imitate the journalism which describes him.

Walter Lippmann

It has been said that politicians should have their ears full of grasshoppers, a result of keeping their ears close to the ground.

George Will

My deepest feeling about politicians is that they are dangerous lunatics to be avoided when possible and carefully humored: people, above all, to whom we must never tell the truth.

W.H. Auden

I know that if one waits for the politician to find a solution, it is almost always the wrong one because politicians, by defnition, react to headlines. And that's always treating the symptoms and leaving the basic conditions untouched.

Peter Drucker

God and the politicians willing, the United States can declare peace upon the world and win it.

Ely Culbertson

Probably the most distinctive characteristic of the successful politician is selective cowardice.

Richard Harris

Take our politicians: they're a bunch of yo-yos. The presidency is now a cross between a popularity contest and a high school debate, with an encyclopedia of cliches as the first prize.

Saul Bellow

His words leap across rivers and mountains, but his thoughts are still only six inches long.

E.B. White

When attacked, politicians are expected to strike back and to seek friends from among the enemies of their enemies.

Editorial in Fortune magazine

Politicians act as though they thought the will of the people is a document bequeathing them something.

John W. Raper

The politicians of our time might be characterized by their vain attempts to change the world and by their inability to change themselves.

George Faludy

The professional politician woos the fickle public more as a man engaged than married, for his is a contract that must be renewed every few years, and the memory of the public is short.

J.T. Salter

Politicians make strange bedfellows, but they all share the same bunk.

Edgar A. Shoaff

One who likes what the majority likes.

Eugene E. Brussell

Politicians who vote huge expenditures to alleviate problems get re-elected; those who propose structural changes to prevent problems get early retirement.

John McClaughry

Politics unfortunately abounds in shams that must be treated reverentially by every politician who would succeed.

James Truslow Adams

A politician weakly and amiably in the right, is no match for a politician tenaciously and pugnaciously in the wrong.

Edwin Percy Whipple

Men play at being God, but lacking God's experience they wind up as politicians.

Harry William King

Some politicians repair their fences by hedging.

Hawley R. Everhart

If we meet an honest and intelligent politician, a dozen, a hundred, we say they aren't like politicians at all, and our category of politicians stays unchanged; we know what politicians are like.

Randall Jarrell

Politicians take no interest in eugenics because the unborn have no vote.

William R. Inge

Politicians are good at distributing pleasure, not at allocating pain.

Christine Olsenius

The wise and clever politician makes the passions and prejudices of his constituents one of his principal assets. Nearly all people vote not according to their own best interests as decided by calm and logical reasons, but according to their passions and prejudices.

J.H. Wallis

The Statesmen

When you're abroad you're a statesman; when you're home you're just a politician.

Harold Macmillan

It is amazing how wise statesmen can be when it is ten years too late.

David Lloyd George

A politician is a person with whose politics you don't agree. If you agree with him he is a statesman.

David Lloyd George

His life has been one great Appropriations Clause. He is a burglar of others' intellects. . . . There is no statesman who has committed petty larceny on so great a scale.

Benjamin Disraeli
on then Prime Minister Robert Peel

A statesman is a politician who places himself at the service of the nation. A politician is a statesman who places the nation at his service.

Georges Pompidou

A statesman is a politician who's been dead for ten or fifteen years.

Harry S. Truman

A statesman is a successful politician who is dead.

Thomas B. Reed

Now I know what a statesman is; he's a dead politician. We need more statesmen.

Bob Edwards

The first requirement of a statesman is that he be dull. This is not always easy to achieve.

Dean Acheson

A politician is a statesman who approaches every question with an open mouth.

Adlai Stevenson

A statesman is any politician it's considered safe to name a school after.

Bill Vaughn

When you're out of office, you can be a statesman.

John Connally

The statesman shears sheep, the politician skins them.

Austin O'Malley

A politician thinks of the next election; a statesman, of the next generation.

James Freeman Clarke

A statesman makes the occasion, but the occasion makes the politician.

G.S. Hilliard

Before you can become a statesman you first have to get elected. And to get elected you have to be a politician, pledging support for what the voters want.

Margaret Chase Smith

I am not an elder statesman. I hate elder statesmen. I am a Democrat and a politician and I'm proud of it.

Harry S. Truman

The Unattributed

A politician is an animal who can sit on a fence and yet keep both ears to the ground.

The experienced politician can toss his hat in the ring and still talk through it.

If a politician tries to buy votes with private money, he is a dirty crook; but if he tries to buy them with the people's own money, he's a great liberal.

He's the kind of a politician who follows you through a revolving door and then comes out ahead of you.

A politician divides his time between passing laws and helping friends evade them.

A politician's opinions are subject to change, all except the one he has of himself.

A politician is a man who stands for what he thinks other people will fall for.

Politicians are of two classes — the appointed and the disappointed.

A successful politician's first commandment: Thou shalt not commit thyself.

Politician: one who is willing to do anything on earth for the workers except become one.

POLITICS

Politics is the most hazardous of all professions. There is no other in which a man can hope to do so much good to his fellow creatures—and neither is there any in which, by a mere loss of nerve, he may do as widespread harm. There is not another in which he may so easily lose his soul, nor is there another in which a positive and strict veracity is so difficult. But danger is the inseparable companion of honor. With all its temptations and degradations that beset it, politics is still the noblest career a man can choose.

Andrew Oliver

The Politicians

The political world is stimulating. It's the most interesting thing you can do. It beats following the dollars.

John F. Kennedy

I used to say that politics was the second oldest profession, and I have come to know that it bears a gross similarity to the first.

Ronald Reagan

Politics is such a torment that I would advise every one I love not to mix with it.

Thomas Jefferson

The excitement of politics got into my veins. . . . I knew how to say "no," but seldom could bring myself to say it. A woman and a politician must say that word often, and mean it—or else.

James J. Walker

Politics is like roller skating. You go partly where you want to go, and partly where the damned things take you.

Henry Ashurst

Being in politics is like being a football coach. You have to be smart enough to understand the game . . . and dumb enough to think it's important.

Eugene McCarthy

Politics is like football. It you see daylight, go through the hole.

John F. Kennedy

A little vagueness goes a long way in this business.

Edmund Brown

If you're in politics and you can't tell when you walk into a room who's for you and who's against you, then you're in the wrong line of work.

Lyndon B. Johnson

I seldom think of politics more than eighteen hours a day.

Lyndon B. Johnson

My daddy told me that if I didn't want to get shot at, I should stay off the firing lines. This is politics.

Lyndon B. Johnson

Dirksen's Three Laws of Politics. (1) Get elected. (2) Get re-elected. (3) Don't get mad, get even.

Everett McKinley Dirksen

There are only two kinds of politics . . . the politics of fear and the politics of trust. One says: you are encircled by monstrous danger . . . the other says the world is a baffling and hazardous place, but it can be shaped to the will of men.

Edmund Muskie

There is no such thing as politics; politics are one form of business, and must be treated strictly as a business.

Mark Hanna

Sometimes in politics one must duel with skunks but no one should be fool enough to allow the skunks to choose the weapons.

Joseph G. Cannon

Politics ought to be the part-time profession of every citizen.

Dwight David Eisenhower

A man who is not interested in politics is not doing his patriotic duty toward maintaining the constitution of the United States.

Harry S. Truman

It is not the man who sits by his fireside reading his evening paper, and saying how bad are politics and politicians, who will ever do anything to save us; it is the man who goes out into the rough hurly-burly of the caucus, the primary, and the political meeting, and there faces his fellows on equal terms.

Theodore Roosevelt

. . . Politics, an art more readily acquired by association than by study.

James F. Byrnes

When someone with a rural accent says, "I don't know anything about politics," zip up your pockets.

Donald Rumsfeld

Politics is not a good location or vocation for anyone lazy, thin-skinned or lacking a sense of humor.

John Bailey

Politics is the art of putting people under obligation to you.

Jake Arvey

I have explained how to succeed in politics. I want to add that no matter how well you learn to play the political game, you won't make a lastin' success of it if you're a drinking man.

George Washington Plunkitt

Politics at its best is the joining and resolving of hard choices; not the coalescing of convenient solutions.

Richard Lamm

The purification of politics is an iridescent dream. Government is force.

John J. Ingalls

Politics is like a Brahma's horns . . . a point here . . . a point there . . . and a lot of bull in between.

Ruth Fountain

Politics and Bedfellows

True it is that politics makes strange bedfellows.

Charles Dudley Warner

Politics does not make strange bedfellows. It only seems that way to those who have not been following the courtship.

Kirkpatrick Sale

Politics makes estranged bedfellows.

Goodman Ace

Bedfellows make strange politics.

Larry K. Smith

The Media

There comes a time when even the reformer is compelled to face the fairly widespread suspicion of the average man that politics is an exhibition in which there is much ado about nothing.

Walter Lippmann

One of the most curious things about politics in America is the extraordinary lack of knowledge concerning its practice and principles not only on the part of the people as a whole but of the practitioners themselves.

Frank R. Kent

The element of fate or accident is what makes politics such a ridiculously intriguing business. It is supposed to be governed by rigid rules, but somebody or something is always intervening to change the game, and even the normal reactions to human conduct somehow fail to apply to presidential candidates.

James Reston

In politics, as in love, timing and luck are fundamental.

James Reston

Politics is like booze and women: dangerous but incomparably exciting.

James Reston

Politics is sex in a hula-hoop.

Richard Reeves

Experience suggests that the first rule of politics is never to say never. The ingenious human capacity for maneuver and compromise make acceptable tomorrow what seems outrageous or impossible today.

William V. Shannon

. . . Politics has a way of putting old wine in new bottles.

David Broder

THE WIT AND WISDOM OF POLITICS

Politics, like nature, abhors a vacuum . . .

David Broder

Politics is a flexible art; the minute you take a fixed position you're in trouble.

Norman Mailer

If we could harness the destructive energy of disagreements over politics, we wouldn't need the bomb.

Barbara Walters

The difference between the men and boys in politics is, and always has been, that boys want to be something, while the men want to do something.

Eric Sevareid

Corruption of politics has nothing to do with the morals, or the laxity of morals, of various political personalities. Its cause is altogether a material one.

Emma Goldman

A political war is one in which everyone shoots from the lip.

Raymond Moley

Politics in its more primitive and vigorous manifestation is not a game or a sport, but a form of civil war, with only lethal weapons barred.

John W. Dafoe

Other Writers

A man known to us only as a celebrity in politics or in trade, gains largely in our esteem if we discover that he has some intellectual taste or skill.

Ralph Waldo Emerson

There is a certain satisfaction in coming down to the lowest ground of politics, for we get rid of cant and hypocrisy.

Ralph Waldo Emerson

Politics is the gizzard of society, full of guts and gravel.

Henry David Thoreau

In politics, it seems retreat is honorable if dictated by military considerations and shameful if even suggested for ethical reasons.

Mary McCarthy

In politics, familiarity doesn't breed contempt. It breeds voters.

Paul Lazarfeld

Life somehow finds a way of transcending politics.

Norman Cousins

Politics is the diversion of trivial men who, when they succeed at it, become important in the eyes of more trivial men.

George Jean Nathan

The attempt to turn a complex problem of the head into a simple moral question for the heart to answer, is of course a necessary part of all political discussions.

Frank Moore Colby

The world of politics is always twenty years behind the world of thought.

John Jay Chapman

Some of 'em want to be kissed and some want you to talk politics . . . but the principle's the same.

H. Granville-Barker

Until you've been in politics you've never really been alive. It's rough and sometimes dirty, and it's always hard work and tedious details, but it's the only sport for grownups—all other games are for kids.

Robert A. Heinlein

Modern politics is, at bottom, a struggle, not of men but of forces.

Henry Adams

Politics, as practiced, whatever its professions, has always been the systematic organization of hatreds.

Henry Adams

Practical politics consists in ignoring facts.

Henry Adams

Politics is not the art of the possible. It consists in choosing between the disastrous and the unpalatable.

John K. Galbraith

Few things are as immutable as the addiction of political groups to the ideas by which they have once won office.

John K. Galbraith

THE WIT AND WISDOM OF POLITICS

Nothing is so admirable in politics as a short memory.

John K. Galbraith

If you can't deliver the pie in the sky you promised, you'd better redefine the pie.

Paul A. Samuelson

Politics is far more complicated than physics.

Albert Einstein

Politics offers yesterday's answers to today's problems.

Marshall McLuhan

I . . . regard the exaggerated hopes we attach to politics as the curse of our age, just as I regard moderation as one of our vanishing virtues.

Irving Kristol

We cannot safely leave politics to politicians, or political economy to college professors.

Henry George

Politics is not all economics, but it is better illuminated by reference to that science than to any other. Certainly without economics, politics is an utter mystery.

Charles A. Beard

There are no political panaceas—except in the imagination of political quacks.

Francis Parkman

Our national politics has become a competition for images or between images, rather than between ideals.

Daniel Boorstin

Political language—and with variations this is true of all political parties, from Conservatives to Anarchists—is designed to make lies sound truthful and murder respectable.

George Orwell

Some Other Observations

Politics is the gentle art of getting votes from the poor and campaign funds from the rich, by promising to protect each from the other.

Oscar Ameringer

Politics is the science of how who gets what, when and why.

Sidney Hillman

Power politics is the diplomatic name for the law of the jungle.

Ely Culbertson

[Politics]. A perpetual emergency.

Ralph Roeder

Politics, like economics, has its own law, independent of morals.

Benedetto Croce

The tool of politics (which frequently becomes its objective) is to extract resources from the general taxpayer with minimum offense and to distribute the proceeds among innumerable claimants in such a way as to maximize support at the polls.

James Schlesinger

In politics you can often be wrong, but never in doubt.

Anonymous

Nothing can be said about our politics that hasn't already been said about hemorrhoids.

Anonymous

To err is human; to blame it on the other party is politics.

Anonymous

The Humorists

This country has gotten where it is in spite of politics, not by the aid of it. That we have carried as much political bunk as we have and still survived shows we are a super nation.

Will Rogers

The short memories of American voters is what keeps our politicians in office.

Will Rogers

I love a dog. He does nothing for political reasons.

Will Rogers

My pollertics, like my religion, being of exceedin' accommodatin' character.

Artemus Ward

There are no friends at cards or world politics.

Finley Peter Dunne

Some insomniacs take this or that potion. Our favorite soporific is the announcement by some official that this or that department will be run without regard to politics.

Franklin P. Adams

Politics, as hopeful men practice it in the world, consists mainly of the delusion that a change in form is a change in substance.

H.L. Mencken

The whole aim of practical politics is to keep the populace alarmed (and hence clamorous to be led to safety) by an endless series of hobgoblins.

H.L. Mencken

The Prime Ministers and Other Englishmen

Politics is the skilled use of a blunt weapon.

Lester Pearson

In politics there is no honor.

Benjamin Disraeli

In politics nothing is contemptible.

Benjamin Disraeli

Real politics are the possession and distribution of power.

Benjamin Disraeli

There is no gambling like politics.

Benjamin Disraeli

Politics are like a labyrinth, from the inner intricacies of which it is even more difficult to find the way of escape, than it was to find the way into them.

William Gladstone

Surely politics open up a great field for the natural man. Self-seeking, pride, domination, power—all these passions are gratified in politics.

William Gladstone

Politics are almost as exciting as war, and quite as dangerous. In war, you can only be killed once, but in politics many times.

Winston S. Churchill

It would be a great reform in politics if wisdom could be made to spread as easily and rapidly as folly.

Winston S. Churchill

What do you want to be a sailor for? There are greater storms in politics than you'll ever find at sea. Piracy, broadsides, blood on the decks— you'll find them all in politics.

David Lloyd George

You will find in politics that you are much exposed to the attribution of false motives. Never complain and never explain.

Stanley Baldwin

The optimist view of politics assumes that there must be some remedy for every political ill, and rather than not find it, it will make two hardships to cure one.

Lord Salisbury

The commonest error in politics is sticking to the carcass of dead policies.

Lord Salisbury

Politics is a blood sport.

Aneurin Bevan

I have never regarded politics as the arena of morals. It is the arena of interests.

Aneurin Bevan

It was a storm in a tea cup, but in politics we sail in paper boats.

Harold Macmillan

The drama of political life oscillates between tragedy and comedy. Indeed it is in the interplay of these that much of the human interest lies. From time to time, to the general amazement of the spectators, it degenerates into melodrama or even farce.

Harold Macmillan

A week is a long time in politics.

Sir Harold Wilson

The reason I am in politics is because I believe in certain things and try to put them into practice.

Margaret Thatcher

One of the difficulties of politics is that politicians are shocked by those who are really prepared to let their thinking reach any conclusion. Political thinking consists in deciding on the conclusion first and then finding good arguments for it. An open mind is considered irresponsible—and perhaps it really is.

Richard Crossman

Politics is the art of looking for trouble, finding it everywhere, diagnosing it wrongly, and applying unsuitable remedies.

Sir Ernest Benn

In politics you have to give the electorate a tune they can whistle.

Enoch Powell

Politics is the art of running human society. Like all art it is continuously changing. Like all art it is the expression of man under the influence of his environment. Politics does not end with the achievement of certain goals or the passing of particular legislation.

Joseph Grimond

In politics, guts is all.

Barbara Castle

Politics is a field where action is one long second best and where the choice constantly lies between two blunders.

John Morley

Most mistakes in politics arise from flat and invincible disregard of the plain maxim that it is possible for the same thing to be and not be.

John Morley

The British Men and Women of Letters

Politics are now nothing more than a means of rising in the world.

Samuel Johnson

Why, Sir, most schemes of political improvement are very laughable things.

Samuel Johnson

Politics is perhaps the only profession for which no preparation is thought necessary.

Robert Louis Stevenson

In politics, what begins in fear usually ends in folly.

Samuel Taylor Coleridge

Politics, as the word is commonly understood, are nothing but corruptions.

Jonathan Swift

Vain hope to make man happy by politics.

Thomas Carlyle

In politics, as in religion, it so happens that we have less charity for those who believe the half of our creed, than for those that deny the whole of it.
Charles Caleb Colton

Politics are not my concern. . . . They impressed me as a dog's life without a dog's decencies.
Rudyard Kipling

The standard of intellect in politics is so low that men of moderate mental capacity have to stoop in order to reach it.
Hilaire Belloc

The nauseous sham goodfellowship our democratic public men get up for shop use.
George Bernard Shaw

Political necessities sometimes turn out to be political mistakes.
George Bernard Shaw

From politics, it was an easy step to silence.
Jane Austen

The results of political changes are hardly ever those which their friends hope or their foes fear.
Thomas Henry Huxley

In our age there is no such thing as keeping out of politics. All issues are political issues, and politics itself is a mass of lies, evasions, folly, hatred and schizophrenia.
George Orwell

Politics are usually the executive expression of human immaturity.
Vera Brittain

Political principles resemble military tactics; they are usually designed for a war which is over.
Richard Tawney

Half a truth is better than no politics.
G.K. Chesterton

A heavy and cautious responsibility of speech is the easiest thing in the world; anybody can do it. That is why so many tired, elderly and wealthy men go in for politics.
G.K. Chesterton

It is now known . . . that men enter local politics solely as a result of being unhappily married.

C. *Northcote Parkinson*

Politics is the art of human happiness.

Herbert Albert Fisher

If you use words for political purposes, they soon lose whatever meaning they may have had.

Charles P. Snow

The great qualities, the imperious will, the rapid energy, the eager nature fit for a great crisis are not required—are impediments—in common times.

Walter Bagehot

Politics and religion are the easiest to hand and the cheapest ways of feeling worth-while and unbored. Thus, a man may be induced to go to chapel or meeting or demonstration for reasons which have nothing to do with morality. . . . Political organisation has the double charm of being in the "gang" which all children want to be and which the adult must often forgo . . .

Naomi Mitchison

It rarely pays in politics to be wise before the event.

Christopher Patten

In politics it is important to know what it feels like to be someone else. . . . Human beings are not islands, least of all politicians.

Sir Edward Boyle

There are too many men in politics and not enough elsewhere.

Hermione Gingold

[Politics] It is completely unimportant. That is why it is so interesting.

Agatha Christie

The Greeks

The good of man must be the end of the science of politics.

Aristotle

Political society exists for the sake of noble actions and not of mere companionship.

Aristotle

They are wrong who think that politics is like an ocean voyage or a military campaign, something to be done with some particular end in view, something which leaves off as soon as that end is reached. It is not a public chore, to be got over with. It is a way of life. It is the life of a domesticated political and social creature who is born with a love for public life, with a desire for honor, with a feeling for his fellows; and it lasts as long as need be.

Plutarch

Here each individual is interested not only in his own affairs but in the affairs of the state as well: even those who are mostly occupied with their own business are extremely well-informed on general politics—this is a peculiarity of ours.

Pericles

The French

One would risk being disgusted if one saw politics, justice and one's dinner in the making.

Nicholas Chamfort

Men ought not to suffer from disenchantment. They ought to know that ideals in politics are never realized.

Jean Pecquet

The body politic, like the human body, begins to die from its birth, and bears in itself the causes of its destruction.

Jean-Jacques Rousseau

In politics nothing is just save what is honest; nothing is useful except what is just.

Robespierre

Most men, in politics as in everything, attribute the results of their imprudence to the firmness of their principles.

Benjamin Constant

In politics a community of hatred is almost always the foundation of friendships.

Alexis de Tocqueville

I have always noticed in politics how often men are ruined by having too good a memory.

Alexis de Tocqueville

Politics is the art of preventing people from taking part in affairs which properly concern them.

Paul Valéry

In politics it is necessary either to betray one's country or the electorate. I prefer to betray the electorate.

Charles de Gaulle

Politics, and the fate of mankind, are shaped by men without ideals and without greatness. Men who have greatness within them don't go in for politics.

Albert Camus

In politics one must take nothing tragically and everything seriously.
Adolphe Thiers

Politics is a systematic effort to move other men in pursuit of some design.

Bertrand de Jouvenel

The Germans

Politics is the doctrine of the possible, the attainable.

Otto von Bismarck

Politics ruins the character.

Otto von Bismarck

Politics is the art of the next best.

Otto von Bismarck

The art of politics consists in knowing precisely when it is necessary to hit an opponent slightly below the belt.

Konrad Adenauer

Only he has the calling for politics who is sure that he will not crumble when the world from his point of view is too stupid or base for what he wants to offer. Only he who in the face of all this can say "In spite of all!" has the calling for politics.

Max Weber

The field of politics always presents the same struggle. There are the Right and the Left, and in the middle is the Swamp.

August Bebel

Other Comments from Around the World

Politics is the art of acquiring, holding and wielding power.

Indira Gandhi

Freedom is not for the timid. If one wishes to be in politics, one must be ready to face all eventualities.

Vijaya Lakshmi Pandit

[Politics]. A rotten egg; if broken open, it stinks.

Russian proverb

There are no morals in politics; there is only expedience. A scoundrel may be of use to us just because he is a scoundrel.

V.I. Lenin

In politics, as in high finance, duplicity is regarded as a virtue.

Mikhail Bakunin

In politics habits, and not only good ones, but bad ones just as well, rule humanity.

Thomas Masaryk

We cannot change our policy now. After all, we are not political whores.

Benito Mussolini

Politics have no relation to Morals.

Niccolò Machiavelli

Final Quotes

Public life is regarded as the crown of a career, and to young men it is the worthiest ambition. Politics is still the greatest and most honorable adventure.

John Buchan (Lord Tweedsmuir)

With all the temptations and degradations that beset it, politics is still the noblest career that any man can choose.

Frederick Scott Oliver

POLLS

For a public opinion pollster, predicting election results is a thankless task. Get the results right and only your mother remembers; make a mistake and you hear about it for years. . . . I guess I'm a glutton for punishment.

Barry Sussman

THE WIT AND WISDOM OF POLITICS

Public opinion pollsters are people who count the grains of sand in your bird cage and then try to tell you how much sand there is on the beach.

Fred Allen

Polls give some politicians, weaker ones, more information than is good for them, particularly if they can't resist the temptation to follow the 51 percent of their district who seemed to be against the Bill of Rights between Tuesday and Thursday of last week.

Richard Reeves

Do you ever get the feeling that the only reason we have elections is to find out if the polls were right?

Robert Orben

Politicians' Rules. (1) When the polls are in your favor, flaunt them. (2) When the polls are overwhelmingly unfavorable, (a) ridicule and dismiss them or (b) stress the volatility of public opinion. (3) When the polls are slightly unfavorable, play for sympathy as a struggling under-dog. (4) When too close to call, be surprised at your own strength.

Paul Dickson
The Official Rules

Don't worry about polls—but if you do, don't admit it.

Rosalynn Carter

These polls that the Republican candidate is putting out are like sleeping pills designed to lull the voters into sleeping on election day. You might call them "sleeping polls."

Harry S. Truman

The opinion polls that are now favouring the coalition parties in the election campaign will only stiffen our opponents to double their efforts. They can have a very counter-productive effect. My warning to our organisers is just to read them—then get on with the job. It's like competition golf; you keep your eye on the ball and don't watch the crowd.

John Douglas Anthony

There is as much difference between an opinion poll and an election as between shooting blank cartridges and live ones.

France-Soir

You can't live or die by polls. I didn't live euphorically at 86 percent nor am I wringing my hands now.

George Bush

PORK BARREL

I don't care what the piece of equipment is—or how bad it is—if it's done in his state, the senator has to stand up and scream for it.

Barry Goldwater

The people of West Virginia don't need a lobbyist. They have me.

Robert C. Byrd

Every time these damn Yankees get a hambone, I'm going to get a hog.

John Nance Garner

Pork barrel spelled backwards is infrastructure.

James Howard

One person's pork barrel project is another person's wise investment in the local infrastructure.

Thomas Foley

POWER

The lust for power, for dominating others, inflames the heart more than any other passion.

Tacitus

Power gradually extirpates from the mind every human and gentle virtue.

Edmund Burke

Unlimited power is apt to corrupt the minds of those who possess it; and this I know, my Lords, that where law ends, tyranny begins.

William Pitt (the Elder)

Power tends to corrupt, and absolute power corrupts absolutely. Great men are almost always bad men, even when they exercise infuence, and not authority. . . . There is no worse heresy than that the office sanctifies the holder of it.

Lord Acton

Men love power. Give all the power to the many, they will oppress the few. Give all the power to the few, they will oppress the many.

Alexander Hamilton

All men having power ought to be distrusted to a certain degree.

James Madison

THE WIT AND WISDOM OF POLITICS

The arts of power and its minions are the same in all countries and in all ages. It marks its victims; denounces it; and excites the public odium and the public hatred, to conceal its own abuses and encroachments.

Henry Clay

Power when wielded by abnormal energy is the most serious of acts.

Henry Adams

I am more and more convinced that man is a dangerous creature; and that power, whether vested in the many or a few, is ever grasping, and that like the grave, cries "Give, give!"

Abigail Adams

There is a homely adage which runs: "Speak softly and carry a big stick; you will go far."

Theodore Roosevelt

I repeat. . . . All power is a trust; that we are accountable for its exercise; that from the people and for the people all springs, and all must exist.

Benjamin Disraeli

They who are in highest places and have the most power, have the least liberty, because they are most observed.

John Tillotson

Bertrand Russell said that the measure of power is the ability to achieve intended results.

George Will

The fundamental conflicts in human life are not between competing ideas, one "true" and the other "false"—but rather between those who hold power and use it to oppress others, and those who are oppressed by power and seek to free themselves of it.

Thomas Szasz

Whoever has power in his hands wants to be despotic; the craze for domination is an incurable disease.

Voltaire

The purpose of getting power is to be able to give it away.

Aneurin Bevan

Men of power have no time to read; yet the men who do not read are unfit for power.

Michael Foot

Power and Liberty are like Heat and Moisture, where they are well mixt, everything prospers; where they are single, they are destructive.

George Savile

Only he deserves power who every day justifies it.

Dag Hammarskjöld

It may be that this office [of president] has more potential—because it doesn't have overt power—to gain an audience, not for immediate change, but for the sounding of values, a vision of the future.

Mary Robinson

It is not power that corrupts but fear. Fear of losing power corrupts those who wield it, and fear of the scourge of power corrupts those subjected to it.

Daw Aung San Suu Kyi

Seven months ago, I could give a single command and 541,000 people would immediately obey it. Today I can't get a plumber to come to my house.

Norman Schwarzkopf

He [Tip O'Neill] understands so well that all political power is an illusion. If people think you have power, then you have power. If people think you have no power, then you have no power.

Jimmy Breslin

Power is the great aphrodisiac.

Anonymous

It's hard not to define power as reporters do. The common perception of power is people running around seeking it.

Barbara Bush

PRAISE

He that praiseth publickly, will slander privately.

Thomas Fuller, M.D.

Praise is like ambergris: A little whiff of it, and by snatches, is very agreeable; but when a man holds a whole lump of it to your nose, it is a stink, and strikes you down.

Alexander Pope

Flattery is alright, if you don't inhale.

Adlai Stevenson

Sweet praise is like perfume. It's fine if you don't swallow it.

Dwight David Eisenhower

PRECINCTS

Never mind about the country, never mind about the state, never mind about the city, never mind about the ward. You take care of your precinct.

Jake Arvey

You don't win elections on Election Day. You win them by what you do all year round, by the day-to-day goodwill you generate in each precinct.

Jake Arvey

If you can't carry your own precinct you're in trouble.

Calvin Coolidge

The whole State must be so well organized that every Whig can be brought to the polls. So divide the county into small districts and appoint in each a committee. Make a perfect list of the voters and ascertain with certainty for whom they will vote. . . . Keep a constant watch on the doubtful voters and have them talked to by those in whom they have the most confidence. . . . On election days see that every Whig is brought to the polls.

Abraham Lincoln

Don't look down on the politician for never having met a payroll if you never have carried a precinct.

Theodore Sorensen

PRESIDENCY

In America any boy may become President and I suppose that's just the risk he takes.

Adlai Stevenson

When I was a boy, I was told anybody could become President; I'm beginning to believe it.

Clarence Darrow

It's a great country, where anybody can grow up to be president . . . except me.

Barry Goldwater

I do not like broccoli and I haven't liked it since I was a little kid and my mother made me eat it and I'm president of the United States and I'm not going to eat any more broccoli.

George Bush

I don't want to sound sanctimonious about this, but I was elected to govern.

George Bush

I always figured the American public wanted a solemn ass for President, so I went along with them.

Calvin Coolidge

I don't expect to get elected. In fact, I just don't want to get elected. What I want is matching funds.

Hymie Mayer

I am convinced that the office of the President is not such a very difficult one to fill, his duties being mainly to execute the laws of Congress.

George Dewey

Henry Clay said, "I would rather be right than President." It may sound like sour grapes, but I would rather be practically anything than President.

Will Cuppy

Having to choose between the White House and the penitentiary, I'd choose the penitentiary.

William Tecumseh Sherman

My movements to the chair of government will be accompanied by feelings not unlike those of a culprit, who is going to the place of his excecution.

George Washington

No one who ever held the office of president would congratulate a friend on obtaining it.

John Adams

Anyone who wants to become President should have his head examined.

Averell Harriman

I would rather that people should wonder why I wasn't President than why I am.

Salmon Chase

Anybody that wants the presidency so much that he'll spend two years organizing and campaigning for it is not to be trusted with the office.
David Broder

Any American who is prepared to run for President should automatically, by definition, be disqualified from ever doing so.
Gore Vidal

The presidency cannot properly be sought or declined.
Andrew Jackson

If a man starts out to make himself President, he hardly ever arrives.
Harry S. Truman

People think I sit here and push buttons and get things accomplished. Well, I spent today kissing behinds.
Harry S. Truman

A President has to be a politician.
Harry S. Truman

A President needs political understanding to run the government, but he may be elected without it.
Harry S. Truman

The President hears a hundred voices telling him that he is the greatest man in the world. He must listen carefully indeed to hear the one voice that tells him he is not.
Harry S. Truman

Within the first few months I discovered that being President is like riding a tiger. A man has to keep on riding or be swallowed.
Harry S. Truman

I used to wonder when I was a member of the House how President Truman got into so much trouble. Now I am beginning to get the idea. It is not difficult.
John F. Kennedy

Sure, it's a big job—but I don't know anyone who can do it better than I can.
John F. Kennedy

When we got into office, the thing that surprised me most was to find that things were just as bad as we'd been saying they were.
John F. Kennedy

There are no easy matters that will ever come to you as President. If they are easy they will be settled at a lower level.

Dwight David Eisenhower
advice to John F. Kennedy

If ever for a second time I should show any sign of yielding to persuasion [to run for President again] please call in the psychiatrists—or even better, the sheriff.

Dwight David Eisenhower

There are blessed intervals when I forget by one means or another that I am President of the United States.

Woodrow Wilson

The second office of the government is honorable and easy, the first is but a splendid misery.

Thomas Jefferson

In the discharge of the duties of the office there is one rule of action more important than all the others. It consists in never doing anything that some one else can do for you.

Calvin Coolidge

One of the first lessons a president has to learn is that every word he says weighs a ton.

Calvin Coolidge

Ohio claims they are due a President as they haven't had one since Taft. Look at the United States, they haven't had one since Lincoln.

Will Rogers

It troubles many good people, not entirely without reason to watch their dignified chief of state dabbling in politics, smiling on party hacks and endorsing candidates he knows to be unfit for anything but immediate delivery to the county jail.

Clinton Rossiter

He was always the champion of vigorous reform before he became President. He talks fairness and justice noisily but evidently has no fixed idea of what they are. He is ready to sacrifice them to expedience at any time.

Mark Twain

The lure of the Presidency is more than a dream; it is a virus for which there is no known drug except victory. . . . And frequently the victors, although never disparaging the office, rebel and lurch against its confines once it is theirs.

Merriman Smith

I would dare to dispute the integrity of the President on any occasion my country's welfare demanded it. . . . After all, the President of the United States is neither an absolute monarch nor a descendent of a sun goddess.

Harold Ickes

[It also demands] a single minded obsession that can distort people. That's all you think about. That's all you talk about. That's who you're around. That's your schedule. That's your leisure. That's your luxury. That's your reading. I told someone, "The question is not whether I can get elected. The question is can I get elected and not be nuts when I get there." It can twist people.

Walter Mondale

Theodore [Roosevelt], if there is one thing more than another for which I admire you, it is your original discovery of the Ten Commandments.

Thomas B. Reed

Esthetically speaking, Presidential Inaugurations have begun to go the way of the Hollywood biblical epic. Both are afflicted by the national passion for overproducing the simplest of dramas.

Russell Baker

I think the presidency is an institution over which you have temporary custody.

Ronald Reagan

Frankly, I don't mind not being President. I just mind that someone else is.

Edward M. Kennedy

PRESSURE GROUPS

Senators and Congressmen fear to offend large and powerful interests or groups in their states, and their votes are largely moulded by their fear. They may have had financial assistance in their campaigns from these groups, and feel under obligations to help them, or they may want financial assistance in their next fight and fear to offend groups that may damage them politically either by contributing money to the other side or by swinging votes against them.

Frank Kent

The fiction of one vote for one person still is maintained politely in high-school classes in civil government; but men and women who touch practical politics, if only obliquely, know that men and women now may have as many votes in government as they have interests for which they are willing to sacrifice time and thought and money....

... But it is the real government. The ruling classes are those who use their craft societies, medical associations, farm bureaus, labor unions, bankers' associations, women's leagues and the like to influence government. Of course it takes time and intelligence, and a little money, but not much. For fifty dollars a year the average family ought to be able to buy a half a dozen powerful votes in government, each one ten times as powerful as the vote guaranteed by the Constitution.

William Allen White

The exact opposite of democracy is government by pressure groups. This is a government under which special interests, by deals and propaganda, endeavour to exploit the community for their own benefit. For example, everyone ought to have a chance to live in a decent environment. Everybody ought to have a chance to live in a decent home. Those who destroy the environment in order to provide homes, and those who would preserve the environment by refusing to provide homes are equally guilty of pressuring democracy; for they must see that the common good requires both.

Robert M. Hutchins

PRIMARY ELECTIONS

There has been an awful lot of people defeated in primaries. Everybody was running that could get some cards printed. It was a great year for the printers.

Will Rogers

The men who put through the primary law are the same crowd that stand for the civil service blight and they have the same objects in view—the destruction of government by party, the downfall of the constitution and hell generally.

George Washington Plunkitt

Two New Hampshire women discussing the election over the back fence. One asks if the other will vote for presidential candidate X:

Oh, no, I couldn't possibly vote for him. I've only met him four times.

It is an aim of my life to die without having written a column about who will win the New Hampshire primary. But, then, I may be the only journalist who has never been to New Hampshire.

George Will

Now the primary election law threatens to do away with the boss and make the city government a menagerie.

George Washington Plunkitt

PRINCIPLES

I am a man of fixed and unbending principles, the first of which is to be flexible at all times.

Everett McKinley Dirksen

The effectiveness of a politician varies in inverse proportion to his commitment to principle.

Sam Shaffer

It is often easier to fight for principles than to live up to them.

Adlai Stevenson

Mark, the great trouble with you is that you refuse to be a demagogue. You will not submerge your principles in order to get yourself elected. You must learn that there are times when a man in public life is compelled to rise above his principles.

Henry Ashurst
to colleague Mark Smith

Senators who go down to defeat in vain defense of a single principle will not be on hand to fight for that or any other principles in the future.

John F. Kennedy

I would rather be an opportunist and float than go to the bottom with my principles around my neck.

Stanley Baldwin

You can't learn too soon that the most useful thing about a principle is that it can always be sacrificed to expediency.

W. Somerset Maugham

There is nothing so bad or so good that you will not find Englishmen doing it; but you will never find an Englishman in the wrong. He does everything on principle. He fights you on patriotic principles; he robs you on business principles; he enslaves you on imperial principles.

George Bernard Shaw

When a man says he approves of something in principle, it means he hasn't the slightest intention of carrying it out in practice.

Otto von Bismarck

PROBLEMS

Nothing is ever solved; old problems are simply absorbed in new problems.

Ferdinand Lundberg

Politics offers yesterday's answers to today's problems.

Marshall McLuhan

When you see ten troubles rolling down the road, if you don't do anything, nine of them will roll into the ditch before they get to you.

Calvin Coolidge

Solutions to problems create problems.

Loren Eiseley

It isn't that they can't see the solution. It is that they can't see the problem.

G.K. Chesterton

A solved problem creates two new problems, and the best prescription for happy living is not to solve any more problems than you have to.

Russell Baker

For every simple problem, there's a solution that is short, simple . . . and wrong.

H.L. Mencken

There are two problems in my life. The political ones are insoluble and the economic ones are incomprehensible.

Sir Alex Douglas-Home

No problem is so big or so complicated that it can't be run away from.

Charles Schulz

Most government officials are rushing headlong to solve the problems of fifty years ago, with their ears assailed by the sound of snails whizzing by.

Eric Jonsson

Now the problems are new and they require new solutions. One hundred years ago Lincoln said, "As the problems are new, we must disenthrall ourselves from the past." I ask you to look ahead.

John F. Kennedy

You don't have a problem—you just have a decision to make.

Robert Schuller

Everything has been thought of before, but the problem is to think of it again.

Johann Wolfgang von Goethe

When you have got an elephant by the hind legs and he is trying to run away, it is best to let him run.

Abraham Lincoln

[Hubert Humphrey]. A politician with no more solutions than there are problems.

Adlai Stevenson

PROCRASTINATION

Procrastination is the thief of time.

Edward Young

Punctuality is the thief of time.

Oscar Wilde

Nothing is so fatiguing as the eternal hanging on of an uncompleted task.

William James

[Procrastination]. It is putting second things first.

Lyndon B. Johnson

While we are postponing life speeds by.

Seneca

[Procrastination]. Creative avoidance.

Anonymous

Never leave that till to-morrow which you can do today.

Benjamin Franklin

Don't put off till tomorrow what can be enjoyed today.

Josh Billings

Whatsoever thou mayst do to-night defer not till to-morrow.

Miles Cloverdale

Never put off until tomorrow what you can do today; there may be a law against it by then.

Ronald Gadde

There is a maxim, "Never put off till to-morrow what you can do today." It is a maxim for sluggards. A better reading of it is, "Never do to-day what you can as well do to-morrow," because something may occur to make you regret your premature action.

Aaron Burr

Do not put off till tomorrow what can be put off till day-after-tomorrow just as well.

Mark Twain

One of these days is none of these days.

English proverb

Tomorrow is often the busiest day of the week.

Spanish proverb

He who hestitates is last.

Mae West

Anything worth doing well is worth doing slowly.

Gypsy Rose Lee

I won't think of it now. I can't stand it if I do. I'll think of it tomorrow at Tara. Tomorrow's another day.

Margaret Mitchell

PROGRESS

Change is certain. Progress is not.

E.H. Carr

All progress has resulted from people who took unpopular positions.
Adlai Stevenson

Usually, terrible things that are done with the excuse that progress requires them are not really progress at all, but just terrible things.
Russell Baker

All progress is based upon a universal innate desire of every organism to live beyond its means.

Samuel Butler (poet)

Progress, far from consisting in change, depends on retentiveness. . . .
Those who cannot remember the past are condemned to fulfill it.
George Santayana

If you've broken the eggs, you should make the omelette.
Anthony Eden

A capsule description of human "progress." By the time you learn how,
it's too late.
Robert A. Heinlein

PROMISES

Vote for the man who promises least; he'll be the least disappointing.
Bernard Baruch

I don't believe irresponsible promises are good politics. Promise-
peddling and double talk may be expedient and catch some votes from
the unwary and innocent, but promises also have a way of coming home
to roost.
Adlai Stevenson

To promise not to do a thing is the surest way in the world to make a
body want to go and do that very thing.
Mark Twain

Promises are not to be kept, if the keeping of them would prove harmful
to those to whom you have made them.
Cicero

To convince a poor voter by the common argument of promised
reforms is merely to corrupt him with hope.
Charles John Darling

Better break your word than do worse in keeping it.
Thomas Fuller, D.D.

Promises and pie crust are made to be broken.
Jonathan Swift

We promise according to our hopes, and perform according to our fears.
La Rochefoucauld

The best way to keep one's word is not to give it.
Napoleon Bonaparte

I can't work under conditions when I am unable to put into effect what I promised my electorate. . . . I made certain commitments in the elections and must fulfill them. If I can't do it, it is my obligation and duty to refuse the post.

Gavril Popov

PUBLIC OPINION

If we're not careful, to be in public life, you're going to have to be the product of a virgin birth.

Martin Franks

We've got forty speakers, which translates into about two hours of public speaking and three hours of council rhetoric.

Bob Crider

In public life it is sometimes necessary in order to appear really natural to be actually artificial.

Calvin Coolidge

It is never the opinion of the moment, but the potential for opinion change which must preoccupy those who seek to exert political influence.

Leo Bogart

That mysterious independent variable of political calculation, Public Opinion.

Thomas Henry Huxley

Its name is Public Opinion. It is held in reverence. It settles everything. Some think it is the voice of God.

Mark Twain

Public opinion in this country is everything.

Abraham Lincoln

With public sentiment, nothing can fail; without it, nothing can succeed. Consequently he who molds public sentiment goes deeper than he who enacts statutes or pronounces decisions.

Abraham Lincoln

In a free and republican government, you cannot restrain the voice of the multitude. Every man will speak as he thinks.

George Washington

A government can be no better than the public opinion which sustains it.

Franklin D. Roosevelt

Laws that do not embody public opinion can never be enforced.
Elbert Hubbard

Public opinion is stronger than the legislature, and nearly as strong as the ten commandments.
Charles Dudley Warner

Public opinion is the thermometer a monarch should constantly consult.
Napoleon Bonaparte

Public sentiment is to public officers what water is to the wheel of the mill.
Henry Ward Beecher

No minister ever stood, or could stand, against public opinion.
John Wilson Croker

Public opinion's always in advance of the Law.
John Galsworthy

What the multitude says is so, or soon will be so.
Baltasar Gracián

Laws they are not . . . which public approbation hath not made so.
Richard Hooker

Today's public opinon, though it may appear light as air, may become tomorrow's legislation—for better or for worse.
Earl Newsome

Government in the last analysis is organized opinion. Where there is little or no public opinion, there is likely to be bad government, which sooner or later becomes autocratic government.
William L. Mackenzie King

In a democracy, as a matter of course, every effort is made to seize upon and create publick opinion, which is, substantially, securing power.
James Fenimore Cooper

Looking over all the great achievements that have made the last half century illustrious, not one of them would have been effected if the opinions of the West End of London had prevailed.
William Gladstone

Public opinion is a compound of folly, weakness, prejudice, wrong feeling, right feeling, obstinacy, and newspaper paragraphs.
Sir Robert Peel

Public opinion, a vulgar, impertinent, anonymous tyrant who deliberately makes life unpleasant for anyone who is not content to be the average man.

William R. Inge

When the people have no other tyrant, their own public opinion becomes one.

Edward Bulwer-Lytton

This notion that public opinion can and will decide all issues is in appearance very democratic. In practice it undermines and destroys democratic government. For when everybody is supposed to have a judgment about everything, nobody in fact is going to know much about anything. . . . Effective government cannot be conducted by legislators and officials who, when a question is presented, asked themselves first and last not what is the truth and which is the right and necessary course, but "What does the Gallup Poll say?" and "How do the editors and commentators line up?"

Walter Lippmann

What is called public opinion, instead of being the united opinion of the whole community, is usually nothing more than the opinion or voice of the strongest interest or combination of interests, and not infrequently of a small but energetic and active portion of the whole. Public opinion, in a relation to government and its policy, is as much divided and diversified as are the interests of the community; and the press, instead of being the organ of the whole, is usually but the organ of these various and diversified interests respectively, or rather of the parties growing out of them.

John C. Calhoun

Politicians, after all, are not over a year behind Public Opinion.

Will Rogers

The public seldom forgive twice.

Johann Kaspar Lavater

The history of the world is the record of the weakness, frailty and death of public opinion.

Samuel Butler (novelist)

You tell me whar a man gets his corn pone, en I'll tell you what his opinions is.

Mark Twain

It is a high honor to be here with you moulders of public opinion. I must say you've done a wonderful job. I doubt if public opinion has ever been as mouldy as it is today.

Robert Stapp

You will find that out of a dozen people who like something in public improvements one will write a letter about it or say something about it. If they don't like something, eleven out of twelve will tell you that. That seems to be human nature.

Robert Moses

We must get the American public to look past the glitter, beyond the showmanship, to the reality, the hard substance of things. And we'll do it . . . not so much with speeches that will bring people to their feet as with speeches that bring people to their senses.

Mario Cuomo

In America, public opinion is the leader.

Frances Perkins

PUBLIC RELATIONS

Shakespeare, in the familiar lines, divided great men into three classes: those born great, those who achieve greatness, and those who have greatness thrust upon them. It never occurred to him to mention those who hire public relations experts and press secretaries to make themselves look great.

Daniel Boorstin

The purpose of public relations in its best sense is to inform and to keep minds open; the purpose of propaganda in the bad sense is to misinform and to keep minds closed.

John W. Hill

Planned public relations is usually a stepchild of conflict.

Kinsey M. Robinson

The impact of immediacy created by TV has placed a premium not on reflection and reason but on the glib answer and bland statement. The politician is concerned with public relations not with public principles.

Richard B. Morris

PUBLIC TRUST

When a man assumes a public trust, he should consider himself as public property.

Thomas Jefferson

Government is a trust, and the officers of the government are trustees; and both the trust and the trustees are created for the benefit of the people.

Henry Clay

The phrase, "public office is a public trust," has of late become common property.

Charles Sumner

Your every voter, as surely as your chief magistrate, excercises a public trust.

Grover Cleveland

The very essence of a free government consists in considering offices as public trusts, bestowed for the good of the country, and not for the benefit of an individual party.

John C. Calhoun

PUBLICITY

We march through life an' behind us marches th' phottygrafter an' th' rayporther. There are no such things as private citizens.

Finley Peter Dunne

We are living in an age of publicity. It used to be only saloons and circuses that wanted their name in the paper, but now it's corporations, churches, preachers, scientists, colleges and cemeteries.

Will Rogers

Formerly, a public man needed a private secretary for a barrier between himself and the public. Nowadays he has a press secretary, to keep him properly in the public eye.

Daniel Boorstin

Of course I'm a publicity hound. Aren't all crusaders? How can you accomplish anything unless people know what you're trying to do?

Vivien Kellems

Without publicity there can be no public support, and without public support every nation must decay.

Benjamin Disraeli

QUALIFICATIONS

Spoke to a candidate today. He feels that if the nomination should ever accidentally get to a question of ability, he has a splendid chance.

Will Rogers

[His] main qualification for the job was exactly what Chamberlain and Sir Horace Wilson were looking for: he had an infinite capacity for being trodden on without complaint.

Leonard Mosley
on the Earl of Halifax for Foreign Secretary

The one thing besides people that I claim to know is land.

Sam Rayburn

I know exactly how it feels to be told that you can't get the job, even though you know you have the qualifications to get that job. The working people of America have a right to be angry. But my life has taught me this: Anger doesn't solve anything. It builds nothing, but it can destroy everything.

Doug Wilder

QUARRELS

Quarrels would not last long if the fault was only on one side.

La Rochefoucauld

The quarrel is a very pretty quarrel as it stands; we should only spoil it by trying to explain it.

Richard Brinsley Sheridan

In quarreling the truth is always lost.

Publilius Syrus

Above all, avoid quarrels caused by wine.

Ovid

QUESTIONS

To play yankee—to answer a question by asking one.

H.L. Mencken

I can evade questions without help; what I need is answers.

John F. Kennedy

It is better to know some of the questions than all of the answers.

James Thurber

Questions are never indiscreet. Answers sometimes are.

Oscar Wilde

A question not to be asked is a question not to be answered.

Robert Southey

Protagoras asserted that there were two sides to every question, exactly opposite to each other.

Diogenes

It is not every question that deserves an answer.

Publilius Syrus

QUORUM

When Republican Thomas B. Reed of Maine was speaker of the U.S. House of Representatives, he was once approached by a Democratic member of the House who demanded: "What becomes of the rights of the minority?" Speaker Reed no doubt expressed the feelings of legislative leaders, before and since, when he replied:

The right of the minority is to draw its salaries, and its function is to make a quorum.

If you're hanging around with nothing to do and the zoo is closed, come over to the Senate. You'll get the same kind of feeling and you won't have to pay. You watch all these speeches being made and nothing going on at all and you think "Where am I? I can't believe this." But don't worry about it. If there are not many people there, you're lucky because you can't do business without a quorum. As long as there are only three or four people on the floor, the country is in good hands. It's only when you have sixty to seventy in the Senate that you want to be concerned.

Robert Dole

QUOTATIONS

A fine quotation is a diamond on the finger of a man of wit, and a pebble in the hand of a fool.

Joseph Roux

When a thing has been said and well said, have no scruple; take it and copy it.

Anatole France

The wise make proverbs and fools repeat them.

Isaac D'Israeli

The wisdom of the wise and the experience of the ages are perpetuated by quotations.

Benjamin Disraeli

THE WIT AND WISDOM OF POLITICS

It is a good thing for an uneducated man to read books of quotations.
Winston S. Churchill

I often quote myself. It adds spice to my conversation.
George Bernard Shaw

Have you ever observed that we pay much more attention to a wise passage when it is quoted, than when we read it in the original author?
Philip G. Hamerton

One must be a wise reader to quote wisely and well.
Amos Bronson Alcott

Though old the thought oft exprest,
'Tis his at last who says it best.

James Russell Lowell

Next to the originator of a good sentence is the first quoter of it.
Ralph Waldo Emerson

Stay at home in your mind. Don't recite other people's opinions. I hate quotations. Tell me what you know.
Ralph Waldo Emerson

Learn the words and quotes of others. Build your inner sea of knowledge to a vast ocean on which you can sail, do not let it become an empty lake or a muddy little duck pond.
R. Maurice Boyd

The difference between my quotations and those of the next man is that I leave out the inverted commas.
George Moore

The power of quotation is as dreadful a weapon as any which human intellect can forge.
John Jay Chapman

Democracy will not be salvaged by men who talk fluently, debate forcefully, and quote aptly.
Lancelot Hogben

How do people go to sleep? I'm afraid I've lost the knack. I might try busting myself smartly over the temple with the nightlight. I might repeat to myself, slowly and soothingly, a list of quotations beautiful from minds profound; if I can remember any of the damn things.
Dorothy Parker

The surest way to make a monkey of a man is to quote him.
Robert Benchley

He who trains his tongue to quote the learned sages will be known far and wide as a smart-ass.
Preston's Postulate

REFORM

The urge to save humanity is almost always only a false-face for the urge to rule it.
H.L. Mencken

A reformer tries to get into office on a flying machine. He succeeds now and then, but the odds are a hundred to one on the lad that tunnels through.
Finley Peter Dunne

[Th' rayformer] don't understand that people wud rather be wrong an' comfortable thin right in jail.
Finley Peter Dunne

To Hell with reform.
Tammany Hall motto

The fact is that a reformer can't last in politics. He can make a show for awhile, but he always comes down like a rocket. Politics is as much a regular business as the grocery or the dry-goods or the drug business. You've sure got to be trained up to it or you're sure to fail.
George Washington Plunkitt

A reformer is a guy who rides through a sewer in a glass-bottomed boat.
James J. Walker

Reformers, as a group, are not a very attractive group of people. As you get older you recognize that. They are too self-righteous. They feel that they have the call.
Robert Moses

A thousand reforms have left the world as corrupt as ever, for each successful reform has founded a new institution, and this institution has bred its new and congenial abuses.
George Santayana

In practice a reformist party considers unshakable the foundations of that which it tends to reform.

Leon Trotsky

Every abuse ought to be reformed, unless the reform is more dangerous than the abuse itself.

Voltaire

Every reform, however necessary, will by weak minds be carried to an excess, that itself will need reforming.

Samuel Taylor Coleridge

It is essential to the triumph of reform that it should never succeed.

William Hazlitt

Men reform a thing by removing the reality from it, and then do not know what to do with the unreality that is left.

G.K. Chesterton

All reform except a moral one will prove unavailing.

Thomas Carlyle

To reform a man is a tedious and uncertain labor; hanging is the sure work of a minute.

Douglas Jerrold

Let us reform our schools, and we shall find little reform needed in our prisons.

John Ruskin

All reformers, however strict their social conscience, live in houses just as big as they can pay for.

Logan Pearsall Smith

Cautious, careful people, always casting about to preserve their reputation and social standing, never can bring about a reform. Those who are really in earnest must be willing to be anything or nothing in the world's estimation.

Susan B. Anthony

Reformers can be as bigoted and sectarian and as ready to malign each other, as the Church in its darkest periods has been to persecute its dissenters.

Elizabeth Cady Stanton

If we like a man's dream, we call him a reformer; if we don't like his dream, we call him a crank.

William Dean Howells

Reform must come from within, not from without. You cannot legislate for virtue.

Cardinal James Gibbons

An indefinable something is to be done, in a way nobody knows how, at a time nobody knows when, that will accomplish nobody knows what.

Thomas B. Reed

Every reform movement has a lunatic fringe.

Theodore Roosevelt

Unless the reformer can invent something which substitutes attractive virtues for attractive vices, he will fail.

Walter Lippmann

Every reform was once a private opinion, and when it shall be a private opinion again, it will solve the problem of the age.

Ralph Waldo Emerson

My own thought is that reform is like garlic in the dressing; a little bit, as every cook knows, goes a very long way.

James J. Kilpatrick

Whoever fights monsters should see to it that in the process he does not become a monster.

Nietzsche

Intelligent discontent is the mainspring of civilization.

Eugene Debs

If you try to make a big reform you are told you are doing too much, and if you make a modest contribution you are told you are only tinkering with the problem.

Sir Alan Patrick Herbert

The system had to change, and to change the system is hard . . . I must tell you I do not call into question the choice of fundamental reform. As for the fact that it was accompanied by a severe worsening of people's everyday life, I think it was not without miscalculations.

Mikhail Gorbachev

RELIGION
Difference of religion breeds more quarrels than difference of politics.
Wendell Phillips

Politics and the pulpit are terms that have little agreement. No sound ought to be heard in the church but the healing voice of Christian charity.

Edmund Burke

All religions united with government, are more or less inimical to liberty.

Henry Clay

All religions must be tolerated ... every man must get to heaven in his own way.

Frederick the Great

Men will wrangle for religion; write for it; fight for it; die for it; anything but—live for it.

Charles Caleb Colton

The trouble with born-again Christians is that they are an even bigger pain the second time around.

Herb Caen

He was one of the faith chiefly in the sense that the church he currently did not attend was Catholic.

Kingsley Amis

Before Christ came into my life, the realities of the materialistic world had the priority in my daily living.

Manuel Noriega

Although he's regularly asked to do so, God does not take sides in American politics.

George Mitchell

The government must pursue a course of complete neutrality toward religion.

John Paul Stevens

The church must be reminded that it is not the master or the servant of the state, but rather the conscience of the state.

Martin Luther King, Jr.

REPRESENTATIVE GOVERNMENT

The more I see of the representatives of the people, the more I admire my dogs.

Alphonse de Lamartine

Your representative owes you, not his industry only, but his judgment; and he betrays you, instead of serving you, if he sacrifices it to your opinion.

Edmund Burke

Parliament is not a congress of ambassadors from different and hostile interests; which interests each must maintain, as an agent and advocate, against other agents and advocates; but parliament is a deliberative assembly of one nation, with one interest, that of the whole; where, not local purposes, not local prejudices ought to guide, but the general good, resulting from the general reason of the whole. You choose a member indeed, but when you have chosen him, he is not a member of Bristol, but he is a member of parliament.

Edmund Burke

If you fear making anyone mad, then you ultimately probe for the lowest common denominator of human achievement.

James Earl Carter, Jr.

REPUBLICAN PARTY

In this world of sin and sorrow there is always something to be thankful for. As for me, I rejoice that I am not a Republican.

H.L. Mencken

I don't want to be a Republican. I just want to live like one.

Eugene Cervi

It seems to be a law of nature that Republicans are more boring than Democrats.

Stewart Alsop

Republicans have never mastered the knack, as Democrats seem to have, of winking while knifing an opponent's jugular.

James W. Naughton

The elephant has a thick skin, a head full of ivory, and as everyone who has seen a circus parade knows, proceeds best by grasping the tail of his predecessor.

Adlai Stevenson

When Republican speech-makers think they are thinking, they are only re-arranging their prejudices.

Adlai Stevenson

I wish somebody would make a new Republican speech.

Frank McKinney Hubbard

The trouble with the Republican Party is that it has not had a new idea for thirty years.

Woodrow Wilson

Brains, you know, are suspect in the Republican Party.

Walter Lippmann

If Jerry Brown says we have to cut down on big government, that's regarded as a liberal coup. If a Republican says that, he's considered as a first-class sonofabitch.

William Steiger

I don't want to lay the blame on the Republicans for the Depression. They're not smart enough to think up all those things that have happened.

Will Rogers

You can't make the Republican Party pure by more contributions, because contributions are what got it where it is today.

Will Rogers

Generally, a Republican looks down when he walks; a Democrat up. Neither looks ahead.

Roger Rosenblatt

There are enough mistakes of the Democrats for the Republicans to criticize constructively without having to resort to political smears. ... Freedom of speech is not what it used to be in America.

Margaret Chase Smith

When a leader is in the Democratic Party he's a boss; when he's in the Republican Party he's a leader.

Harry S. Truman

The Republican Party either corrupts its liberals or it expels them.

Harry S. Truman

In this new Republican Party liberal Republicans are like opera singers: when they are stabbed they don't die; they sing.

Adlai Stevenson

The function of liberal Republicans is to shoot the wounded after the battle.

Eugene McCarthy

I shall work for the Republican party and call on all women to join me, precisely... for what that party has done and promises to do for women, nothing more, nothing less.

Susan B. Anthony

Republicans no longer worship at the shrine of a balanced budget.

Jack Kemp

In Minnesota, the Republicans are like the lowest form of existence. They don't have much life or vitality at the height of their existence, but they never die.

Eugene McCarthy

Republicans are for both the man and the dollar, but in case of conflict the man before the dollar.

Abraham Lincoln

For a working man or woman to vote Republican this year is the same as a chicken voting for Colonel Sanders.

Walter Mondale

REVOLUTIONS

Revolution, n.
In politics, an abrupt change in the form of misgovernment.

Ambrose Bierce

Those who make peaceful revolution impossible, make violent revolution inevitable.

John F. Kennedy

And I shall earnestly and persistently continue to urge all women to the practical recognition of the old Revolutionary maxim, "Resistance to tyranny is obedience to God."

Susan B. Anthony

Marxists-Leninists used to talk about their "permanent revolution," but as it turns out the only permanent revolution the world has ever seen is the American Revolution.

Jack Kemp

I began revolution with eighty-two men. If I had [to] do it again, I do it with ten or fifteen and absolute faith. It does not matter how small you are if you have faith and plan of action.

Fidel Castro

RULES

It is much more material that there should be a rule to go by than what the rule is, that there may a uniformity of proceeding in business not subject to the caprice of the Speaker or captiousness of the members. It is very material that order, decency, and regularity be preserved in a dignified public body.

Thomas Jefferson
in a parliamentary manual adopted by the House of Representatives

If you're going to play the game properly you'd better know every rule.
Barbara Jordan

Members alibi themselves behind the rules when pretending to be for certain legislation but not really for it; or in a desire to avoid a vote on highly controversial subjects.
Fiorello H. La Guardia

The Committee on Rules, composed as nearly as could be of impregnable members from "safe" districts, was counted upon to keep off the floor bills that would embarrass too many members, bills for which there was vociferous public demand but equally loud opposition, bills of an irresponsible nature that were still hard to vote against.
Tom Wicker

If I let you write substance and you let me write procedure, I'll screw you every time.
John Dingell

It doesn't matter if a cat is black or white, so long as it catches mice.
Deng Xiaoping

SECRETS

When a secret is revealed, it is the fault of the man who confided it.
La Bruyère

If you do not want another to tell your secrets, you must not tell them yourself.
Seneca

If you would keep your secret from an enemy, tell it not to a friend.
Benjamin Franklin

The vanity of being known to be entrusted with a secret is generally one of the chief motives to disclose it.

Samuel Johnson

Little secrets are commonly told again, but great ones are generally kept.

Lord Chesterfield

A good many men and women want to get possession of secrets just as spendthrifts want to get money—for circulation.

George D. Prentice

Another person's secret is like another person's money: you are not so careful with it as you are of your own.

Edgar Watson Howe

Many a deep secret that cannot be pried out by curiosity can be drawn out by indifference.

Sydney J. Harris

SELF-CONFIDENCE

Self confidence is the first requisite to great undertakings.

Samuel Johnson

I wish I was as cocksure of anything as Tom Macaulay is of everything.

Lord Melbourne

I do not object to Gladstone always having the ace of trumps up his sleeve but merely to his belief that God Almighty put it there.

Henry Labouchère

Confidence is simply that quiet assured feeling you have before you fall flat on your face.

Anonymous

The confidence which we have in ourselves engenders the great part of that we have in others.

La Rochefoucauld

No one can make you feel inferior without your consent.

Anna Eleanor Roosevelt

Failure? The possibilities don't exist.

Margaret Thatcher

SELF-IMPORTANCE

It is difficult to esteem a man as high as he wishes to be esteemed.

Vauvenargues

He was like a cock who thought the sun had risen to hear him crow.

George Eliot

We would rather speak badly of ourselves than not talk about ourselves at all.

La Rochefoucauld

We reproach people for talking about themselves; but it is the subject they treat best.

Anatole France

We talk little, if we do not talk about ourselves.

William Hazlitt

SEPARATION OF POWERS

When the legislative and executive powers are united in the same person, or in the same body of magistrates, there can be no liberty; because apprehensions may arise, lest the same monarch or senate should enact tyrannical laws, to execute them in a tyrannical manner. ...

... Again, there is no liberty if the judiciary power be not separated from the legislative and executive. Were it joined with the legislative, the life and liberty of the subject would be exposed to arbitrary control; for the judge would be then the legislator. Were it joined to the executive power, the judge might behave with violence and oppression.

Charles de Montesquieu
De L'Esprit des Lois

The principles of a free constitution are irrecoverably lost, when the legislative power is nominated by the executive.

Edward Gibbon

The judicial power ought to be distinct from both the legislative and executive, and independent upon both, so that it may be a check upon both, as both should be checks upon that.

John Adams

Within these limits the power vested in the American courts of justice of pronouncing a statute to be unconstitutional forms one of the most powerful barriers that have ever been devised against the tyranny of political assemblies.

Alexis de Tocqueville

Oh, if I could only be President and Congress too for just ten minutes.

Theodore Roosevelt

A president without both Houses of Congress back of him doesn't amount to much more than a cat without claws in that place that burneth with fire and brimstone.

Joseph G. Cannon

Though the President is commander-in-chief, Congress is his commander, and, God willing, he shall obey. He and his minions shall learn that this is not a government of kings and satraps, but a government of the people, and that Congress is the people.

Thaddeus Stevens

In the Senate you have friends; in the executive you interface.

Walter Mondale

You can lead the House to order, but you can't make it think.

William Weld

If we are to preserve freedom and keep constitutional government alive in America, it cannot be left to a President and his agents alone to decide what must be kept secret. Congress, if it is to check the abuse of executive power, must retain its right to inquiry and independent judgment.

Frank Church

SHOW BUSINESS AND POLITICS

Actors are like politicians, and politicians are like actors. They both spend time each day contemplating their image. They both have a desire to be loved.

Gore Vidal

Acting is as old as mankind. . . . Politicians are actors of the first order.

Marlon Brando

There is a thin line between politics and theatricals.

Julian Bond

The acting abilities of Mr. Wilson and Mr. Macmillan were such that either could have earned a substantial living and devoted following on the stage of the theatre had he not been called instead to the drama of politics.

Bernard Levin
on two former British prime ministers

Two members of my profession not urgently needed by my profession, Mr. Ronald Reagan and Mr. George Murphy, entered politics, and they've done extremely well. Since there has been no reciprocal tendency in the other direction, it suggests to me that our job is still more difficult than their new one.

Peter Ustinov

I learned a lesson in my former profession. We're saving the best stuff for the last act.

Ronald Reagan

The most important thing in acting is honesty. If you can fake that, you've got it made.

George Burns (attr.)

If you want to see your plays performed the way you wrote them, become president.

Vaclav Havel

Having no Hollywood, our politicians are our stars. Without soap operas, Parliament has become our own pitiful drama. Lacking sitcoms, Question Period has become the national laugh track.

Roy MacGregor

I've wondered how people in positions of this kind . . . manage without having had any acting experience.

Ronald Reagan

SILENCE

Blessed is the man who, having nothing to say, abstains from giving us wordy evidence of the fact.

George Eliot

Silence is the best substitute for brains ever invented.

Henry Ashurst

There is no reply so sharp as silent contempt.

Michel de Montaigne

The stillest tongue can be the truest friend.

Euripides

Silence is wisdom, when speaking is folly.

Thomas Fuller, M.D.

SPEECH

Speech was given to the ordinary sort of men whereby to communicate their mind; but to wise men, whereby to conceal it.

Robert South

Most men make little other use of their speech than to give evidence against their own understanding.

George Savile

Men use thought only to justify their wrong-doings, and speech only to conceal their thoughts.

Voltaire

Men talk only to conceal the mind.

Edward Young

Man does not live by word alone, despite the fact that sometimes he has to eat them.

Adlai Stevenson

Let thy speech be better than silence or be silent.

Dionysius the Elder

Let a fool hold his tongue and he will pass for a sage.

Publilius Syrus

A sage thing is a timely silence, and better than any speech.

Plutarch

Speech is silver, silence is golden.

Persian proverb

It is a great misfortune not to possess sufficient wit to speak well, nor sufficient judgment to keep silent.

La Bruyère

Do you wish people to believe good of you? Don't speak.

Pascal

Nature has given us two ears, but only one mouth.

Benjamin Disraeli

Nature has given man one tongue and two ears, that we may hear twice as much as we speak.

Epictetus

Nothing is often a good thing to say, and always a clever thing to say.
Will Durant

I shall never be old enough to speak without embarrassment when I have nothing to talk about.
Abraham Lincoln

The fellow that says, "I may be wrong, but—" does not believe there can be any such possibility.
Frank McKinney Hubbard

When a man has to make a speech, the first thing he has to decide is what to say.
Gerald Ford

SPEECHES

I sometimes marvel at the extraordinary docility with which Americans submit to speeches.
Adlai Stevenson

Political speaking: The fine art of making deep sounds from the stomach sound like important messages from the brain.
Anonymous

The politicians were talking themselves red, white and blue in the face.
Clare Boothe Luce

The most difficult thing in the world is to say thinkingly what everybody says without thinking.
William Alain

The stump speech, put into cold type, maketh the judicious to grieve. But roared from an actual stump, with arms flying and eyes flashing and the old flag overhead, it is certainly and brilliantly effective.
H.L. Mencken

Why don't th' feller who says, "I'm not a speechmaker," let it go at that instead o' givn' a demonstration?
Frank McKinney Hubbard

Our public men are speaking every day on something, but they ain't saying nothing . . .
Will Rogers

Liberty don't work as good in practice as it does in speeches.
Will Rogers

Before a man speaks it is always safe to assume that he is a fool. After he speaks, it is seldom necessary to assume it.

H.L. Mencken

He gave a fireside speech and the fire went out.

Mark Russell
on Henry "Scoop" Jackson

Here comes the orator, with his flood of words and his drop of reason.

Benjamin Franklin

In oratory the great art is to hide art.

Jonathan Swift

The object of oratory is not truth; but persuasion.

Thomas B. Macaulay

Great oratory is great art, at its best to be reckoned among man's glories. But not without reason, oratory has been called the harlot of the arts, so subject it is to abuse and degradation.

Norman Thomas

Oratory is like prostitution: you must have little tricks.

Vittorio Emanuele Orlando

Another mistake: some young men think that the best way to prepare for the political game is to practice speakin' and becomin' orators. That's all wrong. We've got some orators in Tammany Hall, but they're chiefly ornamental. . . . The men who rule have practiced keepin' their tongues still, not exercising them.

George Washington Plunkitt

Men of few words are the best men.

William Shakespeare

Discretion of speech is more than eloquence.

Francis Bacon

One never repents of having spoken too little, but often of having spoken too much.

Phillipe de Commynes

It is very difficult to make a bad speech out of a short speech.

Anonymous

No man pleases by silence; many please by speaking briefly.

Ausonius

THE WIT AND WISDOM OF POLITICS

Let thy speech be short, comprehending much in few words.

Apocrypha

What orators lack in depth they make up for in length.

Charles de Montesquieu

Speeches measured by the hour die with the hour.

Thomas Jefferson

He can compress the most words into the smallest ideas better than any man I ever met.

Abraham Lincoln

That man has a genius for compressing a minimum amount of thought into a maximum of words.

Winston S. Churchill

A speaker who doesn't strike oil in ten minutes should stop boring.

Anonymous

I take the view, and always have done, that if you cannot say what you have to say in twenty minutes, you should go away and write a book about it.

Lord Brabazon

It usually takes me more than three weeks to prepare a good impromptu speech.

Mark Twain

First learn the meaning of what you say, and then speak.

Epictetus

Think today and speak tomorrow.

Henry George Bohn

Don't quote Latin; say what you have to say, and then sit down.

Duke of Wellington
to new member of Parliament

Three things matter in a speech: who says it, how he says it, and what he says—and, of the three, the last matters the least.

John Morley

My father gave me these hints on speech-making: Be sincere . . . be brief . . . be seated.

James Roosevelt

If you can't baffle them with brilliance, befuddle them with bullshit.

Sousa's Principle of Lecture

Let your speech be always with grace, seasoned with salt.

Colossians 4:16

Be swift to hear, slow to speak, slow to wrath.

James 1:19

Accustomed as I am to public speaking, I know the futility of it.

Franklin P. Adams

Now I lay me back to sleep,
The speaker's dull, the subject's deep.
If he should stop before I wake.
Give me a nudge for goodness' sake.

Anonymous

They talk most who have the least to say.

Matthew Prior

There are certain things which are intolerable when second rate: poetry, music, painting and public speaking.

La Bruyère

There is but one pleasure in life equal to that of being called on to make an after-dinner speech, and that is not being called on to make one.

Charles Dudley Warner

All the great speakers were bad speakers at first.

Ralph Waldo Emerson

The finest eloquence is that which gets things done.

David Lloyd George

His speech was like a tangled chain; nothing impaired, but all disordered.

William Shakespeare

It is terrible to speak well and be wrong.

Sophocles

The speeches of one that is desperate, which are as wind.

Job 6:26

The relationship of the toastmaster to the speaker should be the same as that of the fan to the fan dancer. It should call attention to the subject without making any particular effort to cover it.

Adlai Stevenson

A speech is like a love affair. Any fool can start it, but to end it requires considerable skill.

Lord Mancroft

The speech writers write the draft . . . and the committee here or there works on it and then the President gets it. He takes out the red meat. And then you ask why it doesn't sing.

Unidentified White House aide

The great speakers fill me with despair, the bad ones with terror.

Edward Gibbon

Hubert, a speech to be immortal, doesn't have to be eternal.

Muriel Humphrey

I've never thought my speeches were too long. I enjoyed them.

Hubert Humphrey

SPOUSES

I can trust my husband not to fall asleep on a public platform and he usually claps in the right places.

Margaret Thatcher

A thoughtful husband, the [candidate's] manual said, should squelch any rumors that his wife is running for office because their marriage is on the skids. (Why else would a woman want to be in Congress?)

Bella Abzug

You must have your anchor and your gyroscope, somebody to go home to at the end of the day and speak to in magnificent Shakespearean English or four-letter words, and say, "Let me tell you about the silly sons-of-bitches I got involved with today," or lyrically about someone who just dazzled you.

Alan Simpson

Who knows, somewhere out in this audience may even be someone who will one day follow in my footsteps and preside over the White House as the president's spouse (pause). And I wish him well.

Barbara Bush

As you get older, I think you need to get your arms around each other more.

Barbara Bush

If Nancy Reagan instead of Jane Wyman had been Ronald Reagan's first wife, he would never have gone into politics. Instead, she would have seen that he got all the best parts, he would have won three or four Oscars, and had been a real star.

Jimmy Stewart

I'd like to dispel the myth that when you put a wedding ring on a woman, her brain stops.

Marilyn Quayle

STATISTICS

This thing called statistics was the worst thing that was ever invented. ... We wouldn't know how bad the others were doing if we didn't have statistics.

Will Rogers

There are three kinds of lies: lies, damned lies, and statistics.

Benjamin Disraeli

If you put tomfoolery into a computer, nothing comes out but tomfoolery. But this tomfoolery, having passed through a very expensive machine, is somehow ennobled and no one dares criticize it.

Pierre Gallois

Do not put your faith in what statistics say until you have carefully considered what they do not say.

William W. Watt

Statistics are like alienists—they will testify for either side.

Fiorello H. La Guardia

Any statistic that appears interesting is almost certainly a mistake.

A.S.C. Ehrenberg

Statistics are for losers.

Scotty Bowman

With seasonally adjusted temperatures, you could eliminate winter in Canada.

Robert L. Stansfield

Statistician: A man who draws a mathematically precise line from an unwarranted assumption to a foregone conclusion.

Anonymous

Statistician: one who says that if your head is in the oven and your feet are in the refrigerator, the middle of you, on average, will be okay.

Anonymous

Then there is the man who drowned crossing a stream with an average depth of six inches.

Anonymous

Statistics are like a bikini. What they reveal is suggestive, but what they conceal is vital.

Aaron Levenstein

He uses statistics as a drunken man uses lamp posts—for support rather than for illumination.

Andrew Lang

Figures won't lie, but liars will figure.

Charles H. Grosvenor

I always find that statistics are hard to swallow and impossible to digest. The only one I can ever remember is that if all the people who go to sleep in church were laid end to end they would be a lot more comfortable.

Martha Bowers Taft

SUCCESS

How is it that we so seldom hear of the death of a very successful public man without private satisfaction? We are generally glad. I suppose it is because successful men are generally humbugs.

Samuel Butler (poet)

The best way to get on in the world is to make people believe it's to their advantage to help you.

La Bruyère

There are only two ways of getting on in the world: by one's own industry, or by the weaknesses of others.

La Bruyère

Success or failure lies in the conformity to the times.

Niccolò Machiavelli

Ascend above the restrictions and conventions of the world, but not so high as to lose sight of them.

Richard Garnett

Nothing succeeds like the appearance of success.

Christopher Lasch

SUPREME COURT

No matter whether th' constitution follows th' flag or not, th' supreme court follows th' iliction returns.

Finley Peter Dunne

The people can change Congress but only God can change the Supreme Court.

George W. Norris

... Always an institution of political judgment masquerading as a council of priests.

Theodore White

[The Supreme Court] ... could find a loophole in the Ten Commandments.

Tommie Robinson

It is not our job to apply laws that have not yet been written.

John Paul Stevens

I have a lifetime appointment and I intend to serve it. I expect to die at 110, shot by a jealous husband.

Thurgood Marshall

None of us has gotten where we are solely by pulling ourselves up from our own bootstraps. We got here because somebody—a parent, a teacher, an Ivy League crony or a few nuns—bent down and helped us pick up our boots.

Thurgood Marshall

Having been appointed by a Republican President and being accused now of being a flaming liberal on the court, the Republicans think I'm a traitor, I guess, and the Democrats don't trust me. And so I twist in the wind, I hope, beholden to no one, and that's just exactly where I want to be.

Harry Blackmun

TAX REFORM

Tax reform means don't tax you, don't tax me, tax that fellow behind the tree.

Russell Long

What is a loophole? That is something that benefits the other guy. If it benefits you it's tax reform.

Russell Long

Once you get into tax legislation there is always a majority for "reform" but very seldom a majority—after the special interests have done their work—for any particular reform.

Russell Long

Passing a tax reform bill is like walking through an egg field.

Dan Rostenkowski

When you cross a fair maiden, which is the Senate bill, with a gorilla, which is the House bill, you get a gorilla.

John Danforth
on the 1986 Tax Reform Act

TAXES

When there is an income tax, the just man will pay more and the unjust less on the same amount of income.

Plato

It is the part of a good shepherd to shear his flock, not to flay it.

Tiberius

The art of taxation consists in so plucking the goose as to obtain the largest possible amount of feathers with the smallest amount of hissing.

Jean-Baptiste Colbert

A good prince will tax as lightly as possible those commodities which are used by the poorest members of society; e.g. grain, bread, beer, wine, clothing and all other staples without which human life could not exist.

Erasmus

CHUCK HENNING

'Tis pleasant to observe, how free the present Age is in laying taxes on the next.

Jonathan Swift

Excise—a hateful tax levied upon commodities, and adjudged not by the common judges of property, but wretches hired by those to whom excise is paid.

Samuel Johnson

To tax the community for the advantage of a class is not protection: it is plunder.

Benjamin Disraeli

It was as true . . . as turnips is. It was as true . . . as taxes is. And nothing's truer than them.

Charles Dickens

The Chancellor of the Exchequer is a man whose duties make him more or less of a taxing machine. He is intrusted with a certain amount of misery which it is his duty to distribute as fairly as he can.

Robert Lowe

If you drive a car, I'll tax the street.
If you try to sit, I'll tax the seat.

John Lennon

To tax and to please, no more than to love and to be wise, is not given to man.

Edmund Burke

Idleness and pride tax with a heavier hand than kings and parliaments. If we can get rid of the former, we may easily bear the latter.

Benjamin Franklin

Taxation without representation is tryanny.

James Otis

If Patrick Henry thought that taxation without representation was bad, he should see how bad it is with representation.

Old Farmer's Almanac

Our Constitution is in actual operation; everything appears to promise that it will last; but in this world nothing is certain but death and taxes.

Benjamin Franklin

Death and taxes and childbirth! There's never a convenient time for any of them.

Margaret Mitchell

Do we imagine that our assessments operate equally? Nothing can be more contrary to the fact. Wherever a discretionary power is lodged in any set of men over the property of their neighbors, they will abuse it.

Alexander Hamilton

The delicate duty of devising schemes of revenue should be left where the Constitution has placed it—with the immediate representatives of the people.

William Henry Harrison

I would suggest the taxation of all property equally, whether church or corporation.

Ulysses S. Grant

When more of the people's sustenance is exacted through the form of taxation than is necessary to meet the just obligations of Government and expenses of its economic administration, such exaction becomes ruthless extortion and a violation of the fundamental principles of a free government.

Grover Cleveland

Collecting more taxes than is absolutely necessary is legalized robbery.

Calvin Coolidge

It is not a tax but a tax relief bill providing relief not for the needy but for the greedy.

Franklin D. Roosevelt

Taxes, after all, are the dues that we pay for the privilege of membership in an organized society.

Franklin D. Roosevelt

Taxes are what we pay for civilized society.

Oliver Wendell Holmes, Jr.

An unlimited power to tax involves, necessarily, the power to destroy.

Daniel Webster

The power to tax involves the power to destroy.

John Marshall
McCullough v. Maryland, 1819

The power to tax is not the power to destroy while this court sits.

Oliver Wendell Holmes, Jr.
Panhandle Oil v. Knox, 1928

It looks as if the tax laws are a conspiracy in restraint of understanding.
Howard A. Dawson, Jr.

Today, it takes more brains and effort to make out the income-tax form than it does to make the income.
Alfred E. Neuman

The hardest thing in the world to understand is the income tax.
Albert Einstein

There is something wrong with any law that causes many people to have to take a whole day off their jobs to find out how to comply.
T. Coleman Andrews

Look, just because you don't understand it and I can't explain it doesn't mean it's not a good idea.
Al Ullman

The Income Tax has made more Liars out of the American people than Golf has.
Will Rogers

I ... shall never use profanity except in discussing house rent and taxes. Indeed, upon second thought, I will not even use it then, for it is un-Christian, inelegant and degrading—though to speak truly I do not see how house rent and taxes are going to be discussed worth a cent without it.
Mark Twain

Man is not like other animals in the ways that are really significant: animals have instincts, we have taxes.
Erving Coffman

Count the day won when, turning on its axis,
this earth imposes no additional taxes.
Franklin P. Adams

Some taxpayers close their eyes, some stop their ears, some shut their mouths, but all pay through the nose.
Evan Esar

Next to being shot at and missed, nothing is quite as satisfying as an income tax refund.
F.J. Raymond

A tax cut is the kindest cut of all.
Anonymous

The point to remember is that what the government gives it must first take away.

John S. Coleman

We are compelled to admire the efficiency of the government in assessing and collecting taxes.

William Feather

Never before have so many been taken for so much and left with so little.

Van Panopoulos

[Taxpayer]. One who has the government on his payroll.

Anonymous

The taxpayer—that's someone who works for the federal government but doesn't have to take a civil service examination.

Ronald Reagan

The one thing that hurts more than paying income tax is not having to pay an income tax.

Thomas R. Dewar

Congress should know how to levy taxes, and if it doesn't know how to collect them, then a man is a fool to pay taxes.

J. Pierpont Morgan

Anybody has a right to evade taxes if he can get away with it. No citizen has a moral obligation to assist in maintaining the government. If Congress insists on making stupid mistakes and passing foolish tax laws, millionaires should not be condemned if they take advantage of them.

J. Pierpont Morgan

I'm proud to pay taxes in the United States; the only thing is I could be just as proud for half of the money.

Arthur Godfrey

The modern liberal rallies to protect the poor from taxes which in the next generation, as a result of a higher investment for their children, would eliminate poverty.

John K. Galbraith

People hate taxes the way children hate brushing their teeth—and in the same shortsighted way.

Paul A. Samuelson

Of all debts, men are least willing to pay their taxes; what a satire this is on government.

Ralph Waldo Emerson

War involves in its progress such a train of unforeseen and unsupposed circumstances that no human wisdom can calculate the end. It has but one thing certain and that is to increase taxes.

Thomas Paine

The thing generally raised on city land is taxes.

Charles Dudley Warner

There is just one thing I can promise you about the outer-space program: your dollars will go farther.

Werner von Braun

The Congress will push me to raise taxes, and I'll say no, and they'll push and I'll say no, and they'll push again, and I'll say to them, "Read my lips: no new taxes."

George Bush

If you don't drink, smoke or drive a car, you're a tax evader.

Thomas Foley

THINKING

To most people nothing is more troublesome than the effort of thinking.

Lord James Bryce

There is no expedient to which man will not resort to avoid the real labor of thinking.

Sir Joshua Reynolds

All the problems of the world could be settled easily if men were only willing to think. The trouble is that men very often resort to all sorts of devices in order not to think, because thinking is such hard work.

Thomas J. Watson

If you make people think they're thinking, they'll love you; but if you really make them think, they'll hate you.

Don Marquis

A new thinker is only one who does not know what the old thinkers have thought.

Frank Moore Colby

It is well for people who think to change their minds occasionally in order to keep them clean. For those who do not think, it is best at least to rearrange their prejudices once in a while.

Luther Burbank

A great many people think they are thinking when they are really rearranging their prejudices.

Edward R. Murrow

Yon Cassius has a lean and hungry look;
He thinks too much: such men are dangerous.

William Shakespeare

When a thought is too weak to be expressed simply, it should be rejected.

Vauvenargues

TORIES

If there were no Tories, I am afraid he [Gladstone] would invent them.

Lord Acton

Had they been in the wilderness they would have complained of the Ten Commandments.

John Bright

They have always been wrong; they will always be wrong; and when they cease to be wrong they will cease to be the Tory party.

John Bright

Tories are not always wrong, but they are always wrong at the right moment.

Lady Violet Bonham Carter Asquith

The closest thing to a Tory in disguise is a Whig in power.

Benjamin Disraeli

I am an English Liberal. I hate the Tory party, their men, their words, and their methods.

Winston S. Churchill

A Conservative is only a Tory who is ashamed of himself.

John Hookham Frere

We do not say that the Tories are bad men, or wicked men, or even that we are better men than they. We merely say: they are irrelevant.

Aneurin Bevan

The Tory party survives because it is a comprehensive party, a coalition of classes and interests and temperaments; it is in short a church whereas the Labour party is a sect.

Norman T. St. John-Stevas

When the Tories are in trouble, they bunch together and cogger up. When we [the Labour Party] get into trouble, we start blaming each other and rushing to the press to tell them all the terrible things that somebody else has done.

Richard Crossman

The Labour party is like a stage-coach. If you rattle along at great speed everybody inside is too exhilarated or too seasick to cause any trouble. But if you stop everybody gets out and argues about where to go next.

Sir Harold Wilson

[A] successful Party of the right must continue to recruit from the center and even from the left center. Once it begins to shrink into itself like a snail, it will be doomed.

Harold Macmillan

TRUST

Never trust a man who speaks well of everybody.

John Churton Collins

Trust everybody, but cut the cards.

Finley Peter Dunne

Trust not him with your secrets, who, when left alone in your room, turns over your papers.

Johann Kaspar Lavater

The trust we put in ourselves makes us feel trust in others.

La Rochefoucauld

Trust was a good man, but Trust-not was a better.

Italian proverb

Let me tell you, you can trust the Germans.

Helmut Kohl

TRUTH

I don't mind what the opposition say of me, so long as they don't tell the truth about me; but when they descend to telling the truth about me, I consider that that is taking an unfair advantage.

Mark Twain

THE WIT AND WISDOM OF POLITICS

Often, the surest way to convey misinformation is to tell the strict truth.

Mark Twain

When you want to fool the world, tell the truth.

Otto von Bismarck

As scarce as truth is, the supply has always been in excess of the demand.

Josh Billings

One of the things I have had to learn in life is that in political matters truth prematurely uttered is of scarcely greater value than error.

George F. Kennan

That continuous need for approbation dictates the politician's definition of truth no matter how vociferously he denies it. The truth is that arrangement of facts which makes him look good.

Roderick MacLeish

You can always get the truth from an American statesman after he has turned seventy or given up hope of the Presidency.

Wendell Phillips

I don't have to write down what I say because I always tell the truth.

Harry S. Truman

I never did give anybody hell. I just told the truth and they thought it was hell.

Harry S. Truman

"My dear Mr. Greech," said Lady Caroline, "we all know that Prime Ministers are wedded to the truth, but like other wedded couples they sometimes live apart."

H.H. Munro

Tell the truth, and so puzzle and confound your adversaries.

Sir Henry Wotton

Something unpleasant is coming when men are anxious to tell the truth.

Benjamin Disraeli

Men occasionally stumble over the truth, but most of them pick themselves up and hurry off as if nothing had happened.

Winston S. Churchill

The most awful thing that one can do is to tell the truth. It's all right in my case because I am not taken seriously.

George Bernard Shaw

I speak truth, not so much as I would but as much as I dare; and I dare a little more as I grow older.

Michel de Montaigne

If one cannot invent a really convincing lie, it is often better to stick to the truth.

Angela Thirkell

There are no whole truths; all truths are half-truths. It is trying to treat them as whole truths that plays the devil.

Alfred North Whitehead

Truth is the secret of eloquence and of virtue, the basis of moral authority; it is the highest summit of art and of life.

Henri-Frederic Amiel

If you want to annoy your neighbors, tell the truth about them.

Pietro Aretino

He who speaks the truth must have one foot in the stirrup.

Bruce Babbitt

UNDERSTANDING

If you are sure you understand everything that is going on, you are hopelessly confused.

Walter Mondale

[Marshall McLuhan]. He's not meant to be understood, he's meant to be respected.

Mort Sahl

Poincaré knows everything and understands nothing. Briand understands everything and knows nothing.

David Lloyd George

We live under a system of tacit understandings. But the understandings are not always understood.

Sidney Low

Anyone who isn't confused really doesn't understand the situation.

Edward R. Murrow

VICE PRESIDENTS

The second office of the government is honorable and easy, the first is but a splendid misery.

Thomas Jefferson

My country has in its wisdom contrived for me the most insignificant office that ever the invention of man contrived or his imagination conceived; and as I can do neither good nor evil, I must be borne away by others and meet the common fate.

John Adams

A steppingstone . . . to oblivion.

Theodore Roosevelt

Once there were two brothers. One ran away to sea, the other was elected Vice President, and nothing was heard of either of them again.

Thomas Marshall

The Vice President is like a man in a cataleptic state; he cannot speak; he cannot move; he suffers no pain; and yet he is perfectly conscious of everything that is going on around him.

Thomas Marshall

Worst damfool mistake I ever made was letting myself be elected Vice President of the United States. Should have stuck with my old chores as Speaker of the House. I gave up the second most important job in government for one that didn't amount to a hill of beans. I spent eight long years as Mr. Roosevelt's spare tire. I might still be Speaker if I hadn't let them elect me Vice President.

John Nance Garner

A spare tire on the automobile of government.

John Nance Garner

The Vice Presidency of the United States isn't worth a pitcher of warm spit.

John Nance Garner

The vice presidency is about as useful as a cow's fifth teat.

Harry S. Truman

I have not been calling the signals, I have been in the position of a lineman doing some of the downfield blocking.

Hubert Humphrey

All that Hubert needs over there is a gal to answer the phone and a pencil with an eraser on it.

Lyndon B. Johnson

The best part of being Vice President is presiding over the Senate. Where else could I have Barry Goldwater addressing me as Mr. President?

Nelson Rockefeller

It's not such a bad job. All inside work . . . no heavy lifting.

Walter Mondale

If you want to talk to somebody who's not busy, call the vice president. I get plenty of time to talk to anybody about anything.

Walter Mondale

The Vice Presidency is sort of like the last cookie on the plate. Everybody insists he won't take it, but somebody always does.

Bill Vaughn

The whole trouble with the Vice-Presidential office is that a man who would announce his candidacy for it probably is not big enough to fill it.

William Allen White

I am against vice in every form, including the Vice Presidency.

Morris Udall

There is absolutely no circumstance whatever under which I would accept that spot. Even if they tied and gagged me, I would find a way to signal by wiggling my ears.

Ronald Reagan

THE WIT AND WISDOM OF POLITICS

Vice President Dan Quayle has made his own contributions:

What a waste it is to lose one's mind—or not to have a mind. How true that is.

I love California. I grew up in Phoenix.

Hawaii has always been a very pivotal role in the Pacific. It is in the Pacific. It is a part of the United States that is an island that is right here.

I was recently on a tour of Latin America, and the only regret I have was that I didn't study Latin harder in school so I could converse with these people.

Finally, comedian Mark Russell, participating in a television news panel just prior to the Democrats' 1984 convention, was asked if he thought the party would nominate a woman for Vice President. He responsed:

I think they have more respect for women than to do that. You know how demeaning the office of Vice President is? It's the moral equivalent of barefoot and pregnant.

VICTORY

All victories breed hate, and that over your superior is foolish or fatal.
Baltasar Gracián

A victor need give no explanations. The majority do not look closely into circumstantial detail but only at a successful, or unsuccessful, outcome; thus one's reputation never suffers if one's object is obtained.
Baltasar Gracián

If you live long enough, you'll see that every victory turns into a defeat.
Simone de Beauvoir

VOTING

At the bottom of all the tributes paid to democracy is the little man, walking into the little booth, with a little pencil, making a little cross on a little bit of paper—no amount of rhetoric or voluminous discussion can posssibly diminish the overwhelming importance of the point.
Winston S. Churchill

People vote their resentment, not their appreciation. The average man does not vote for anything, but against something.

William Bennett Munro

Voters quickly forget what a man says.

Richard M. Nixon

It doesn't matter if they knock the wall down when they vote for you or hold their nose. It all counts the same.

Richard M. Nixon

Nobody will ever deprive the American people of the right to vote except the American people themselves—and the only way they could do that is by not voting.

Franklin D. Roosevelt

Let us never forget that government is ourselves and not an alien power over us. The ultimate rulers of our democracy are not a President and senators and congressmen and government offficials, but the voters of this country.

Franklin D. Roosevelt

Your every voter, as surely as your chief magistrate, under the same high sanction, though in a different sphere, exercises a public trust.

Grover Cleveland

The right to vote is the basic right without which all others are meaningless. It gives people—people as indviduals—control over their own destinies.

Lyndon B. Johnson

The ignorance of one voter in a democracy impairs the security of all.

John F. Kennedy

Ask a man which way he is going to vote, and he will probably tell you. Ask him, however, why, and vagueness is all.

Bernard Levin

We go by the major vote, and if the majority are insane, the sane must go to the hospital.

Horace Mann

Voting is simply a way of determining which side is stronger without putting it to the test of fighting.

H.L. Mencken

THE WIT AND WISDOM OF POLITICS

America is a land where a citizen will cross the ocean to fight for democracy and won't cross the street to vote in a national election.

Bill Vaughn

The apathy of the modern voter is the confusion of the modern reformer.

Learned Hand

As long as I count the votes what are you going to do about it?

William M. Tweed

The secret ballot is the most sacred heritage which we have and that I have stood by. Even my wife doesn't know how I voted.

Nelson Rockefeller

One man shall have one vote.

John Cartright

"Vote early and vote often," the advice openly displayed on the election banners in one of our northern cities.

W.P. Miles

All voting is a sort of gaming, like chequers or backgammon, with a slight moral tinge to it.

Henry David Thoreau

The freeman casting, with unpurchased hand,
The vote that shakes the turrets of the land.

Oliver Wendell Holmes

People often say that in a democracy, decisions are made by a majority of the people. Of course, that is not true. Decisions are made by a majority of those who make themselves heard and who vote—a very different thing.

Walter Judd

The man who can right himself by a vote will seldom resort to a musket.

James Fenimore Cooper

A straw vote only shows which way the hot air blows.

O. Henry

Our pathway is straight to the ballot box, with no variableness nor shadow of turning.

Elizabeth Cady Stanton

Whenever a fellow tells me he's bipartisan, I know he's going to vote against me.

Harry S. Truman

WAR

War is much too serious a thing to be left to military men.
Charles-Maurice de Talleyrand-Perigord

It is politics which begets war. Politics represents the intelligence, war merely its instrument, not the other way round. The only possible course in war is to subordinate the military viewpoint to the political. War is nothing more than the continuation of politics by other means. It is not merely a political act but a real political instrument.
Karl von Clausewitz

There is no human activity that stands in such constant and universal contact with chance.
Karl von Clausewitz

We must further expressly and exactly establish the point of view, no less necessary in practice, from which war is regarded as nothing but the continuation of politics by other means.
Karl von Clausewitz

War is a matter not so much of arms as of expenditure, through which arms may be made of service.
Thucydides

The guy that made the bullets was paid five dollars a day and the man that stopped them fifteen dollars a month.
Will Rogers

Frankly, I'd like to see government get out of war altogether and leave this whole field to private industry.
Joseph Heller

I don't mean to be flippant, but there's no nice way to kill somebody in a war.
Pete Williams

Nobody minds a war once in a while if it doesn't last too long, and isn't in your neighborhood.
Bertrand Russell

WASHINGTON, D.C.

The more I observed Washington, the more frequently I visited it, and the more I interviewed there, the more I understood how prophetic L'Enfant was when he laid it out as a city that goes around in circles.

John Mason Brown

One of these days this will be a very great city if nothing happens to it.

Henry Adams

Washington is a Democratic company town. When Democrats come here, they have nowhere better to go back to, so they stay. When Republicans come, they're regarded as a temporary occupying army. They'll go away.

Unidentified Washington social leader

There are a number of things wrong with Washington. One of them is that everyone has been too long away from home.

Dwight David Eisenhower

People only leave by way of the box—ballot or coffin.

Claiborne Pell

Success and prominence are Washington's true transients.

Laurence Leamer

Washington is a city of Southern efficiency and Northern charm.

John F. Kennedy

Washington is a crazy quilt of people who have each other by their vulnerable parts.

Douglass Cater

Washington is called the District of Columbia: Because it's too small to be a state, but too large to be an asylum for the mentally deranged.

Anne Gorsuch Burford

Washington, under Democrats and Republicans, has a profoundly neurotic attitude towards "the people." It is built on equal parts of suspicion, loathing, fear, respect and dependence.

Meg Greenfield

Everybody thinks he can run the place better than anybody.

Merriman Smith

A friend of mine says that every man who takes office in Washington either grows or swells, and when I give a man an office, I watch him carefully to see whether he is swelling or growing.

Woodrow Wilson

CHUCK HENNING

A place where men praise courage and act on elaborate personal cost-benefit calculation.

John K. Galbraith

The real trick in Washington is to keep as unobligated as you can while piling up as many IOUs as possible.

Dan H. Fenn

If you don't know who you are before you get here this is a poor place to find out.

Alan Simpson

The longer the title, the less important the job.

George McGovern

The humorists have had their say about Washington:

... A stud farm for every jackass in the country.

Mark Twain

Now look here, old friend, I know the human race; and I know that when a man comes to Washington, I don't care if it's from Heaven, it's because he wants something.

Mark Twain

It's easy enough to see why a man goes to the poorhouse or the pentitentiary. It's because he can't help it. But why he should voluntarily go and live in Washington is entirely beyond my comprehension.

Artemus Ward

Washington appears to be filled with two kinds of politicians—those trying to get an investigation started, and those trying to get one stopped.

Earl Wilson

The further you get away from Washington, the more you think things are under control there.

Art Buchwald

There are no straight balls pitched back there. They're all curves and sliders.

J. Edgar Chenoweth

Too often our Washington reflex is to discover a problem and then throw money at it, hoping it will somehow go away.

Kenneth Keating

THE WIT AND WISDOM OF POLITICS

Nobody believes a rumor in Washington until it's officially denied.
Edward Cheyfitz

An endless series of mock palaces clearly built for clerks.
Ada Louise Huxtable

Like a giant log floating downstream with a million ants on it. Each one thinks he's steering.
Anonymous

Has been defined as 69.2 square miles surrounded by reality.
Anonymous

The only place where sound travels faster than light.
Anonymous

New directive: If it moves, control it. If you can't control it, tax it. If you can't tax it . . . give it a billion dollars.
Anonymous

Getting action in Washington is like mating elephants; it's done at a high level, with a great deal of roaring and screaming, and it takes two years to produce results.
Anonymous

Washington is a city filled with people who believe they are important.
David Brinkley

This is a town where status shifts so swiftly that a euphoric Powerful Job who never had time to return his phone calls can easily turn into a decompressing Used-To-Be-Close-To whose telephone never rings.
Sondra Gotlieb

The cocktail glass is one of the more powerful instruments of government.
Kenneth Crawford

This is a curious place, people gathered together in little cubicles spending millions of bucks protecting every tree, bird, geese in the field, snails. But give them another human being to gnaw on, and they eat that SOB alive—alive! And they spend time doing it—how to embarrass, how to research, how to investigate, how to get into their personal lives, how to get into their heads. What a game. And meanwhile being assured that we protect wolves and cats and things that are important in life, too. But how about looking at fellow humans first. How about the poor human beings that are left bruised, battered, washed up and can't sleep at night.
Alan Simpson

If the world would only follow Washington's shining example, all human woes would vanish from the face of the earth. But you know how the world is, there's no telling it anything. The fact is, hardly a day goes by but that Congress and the administration, in splendid harmony, demonstrate that there's no problem so great that it must be faced.

Alan Abelson

If you want a friend in Washington, buy a dog.

Harry S. Truman

You can't trust the dogs in this town.

Clarence Thomas

The press is very powerful in Washington. It's the only permanent power in Washington; everything else is transient.

Sondra Gotlieb

Nothing ever gets settled in this town . . . a seething debating society in which the debate never stops, in which people never give up, including me. And so that's the atmosphere in which you administer.

George P. Schultz

This city is nowhere near as important as it thinks it is.

David Brinkley

Make sure you know when you're pretending.

Robert Kerrey

WISDOM

As for me, all I know is that I know nothing.

Socrates

It is a maxim of the wise to leave things before things leave them.

Baltasar Gracián

Wisdom is divided into two parts: (1) having a great deal to say, and (2) not saying it.

Anonymous

It is easier to be wise for others than for ourselves.

La Rochefoucauld

Be wiser than other people if you can, but do not tell them so.

Lord Chesterfield

A man doesn't begin to attain wisdom until he recognizes that he is no longer indispensable.

Richard E. Byrd

The good Lord set definite limits on man's wisdom, but set no limits on his stupidity—and that's just not fair!

Konrad Adenauer

WOMEN IN POLITICS

Politics is not the Business of a Woman.

Mary Manley

Whether women are better than men I cannot say—but I can say they are certainly no worse.

Golda Meir

The things we believe in and want done will not be done until women are in elective office.

Catherine Drinker Bowen

It is time that women took their places in Imperial politics.

Emmeline Pankhurst

My vigor, vitality and cheek repell me. I am the kind of woman I would run from.

Nancy Astor

To put a woman on the [presidential] ticket would challenge the loyalty of women everywhere to their sex, because it would be made to seem that the defeat of the ticket meant the defeat for a hundred years of women's chance to be truly equal with men in politics.

Clare Boothe Luce

In politics women . . . type the letters, lick the stamps, distribute the pamphlets and get out the vote. Men get elected.

Clare Boothe Luce

In politics, if you want anything said, ask a man; if you want anything done, ask a woman.

Margaret Thatcher

One of the things being in politics has taught me is that men are not a reasoned or reasonable sex.

Margaret Thatcher

She is so clearly the best man among them.

Barbara Castle
on Margaret Thatcher

Men never feel at ease with a woman politician who looks as if her hair has just been permed.

Roy Jenkins

Life in the House [of Commons] is neither healthy, useful nor appropriate for a woman; and the functions of a mother and a member are not compatible.

Margot Asquith

... The new woman in politics seems to be saying that we already know how to lose, thank you very much. Now we want to learn how to win.

Gloria Steinem

It certainly must have been a relief for the women of the country to realize that one could be a woman and a lady and yet be thoroughly political.

Agnes Meyer

What the emergence of woman as a political force means is that we are quite ready now to take on responsibilities as equals, not protected partners.

Jill Ruckelshaus

There is no hope even that woman, with her right to vote, will ever purify politics.

Emma Goldman

Who knows what women can be when they finally become free to be themselves.

Betty Friedan

To be successful a woman has to be much better at her job than a man.

Golda Meir

We hold these truths to be self-evident, that all men and women are created equal.

Elizabeth Cady Stanton

There will never be complete equality until women themselves help to make laws and elect lawmakers.

Susan B. Anthony

But if God had wanted us to think with our wombs, why did he give us a brain?

Clare Boothe Luce

Women's issues are people's issues.

Pat Schroeder

Real equality is not going to come when a female Einstein is recognized as quickly as a male Einstein, but when a female schlemiel is promoted as quickly as a male schlemiel.

Bella Abzug

I would rather be thought of as a Latin Margaret Thatcher.

Violeta Chamorro

I've always had the feeling I could do anything; my daddy told me I could, and I was in college before I found out he might be wrong.

Ann Richards

Toughness doesn't have to come in a pinstripe suit.

Dianne Feinstein

Party organization matters. When the door of a smoke-filled room is closed, there's hardly ever a woman inside.

Millicent Fenwick

WRITING

Writing is easy. I just open a vein and bleed.

Red Smith

Writing a newspaper column is like being married to a nymphomaniac. The first two weeks, it's fun.

Lewis Grizzard

Writing is not hard. Just get paper and pencil, sit down, and write as it occurs to you. The writing is easy—it's the occurring that's hard.

Stephen Leacock

I write in longhand, wih a fountain pen, of course. I do so not as a political statement—although a Tory could hardly do otherwise—but because writing should be a tactile pleasure. You should feel sentences taking shape. People who use "word processors" should not be surprised if what they write is to prose as processed cheese is to real cheese.

George Will

CHUCK HENNING

The right to write badly was a privilege widely used.

Isaac Babel

I write to discover what I think.

Daniel Boorstin

If you wish to be a writer, write.

Epictetus

In writing and politicking, it's best not to think about it, just do it.

Gore Vidal

All of us learn to write in the second grade. Most of us go on to greater things.

Bobby Knight

Politics, as it turned out, lent itself admirably to storytelling. Where else can you find such a mix of greed, power, lust, conspiracy, sacrifice and secrecy?

Val Sears

The writer, unless he is a mere word processor, retains three attitudes that power-made regimes cannot tolerate: a human imagination, in the many forms it may take; the power to communicate; and hope.

Margaret Atwood

X-RATED

I never trust a man unless I've got his pecker in my pocket.

Lyndon B. Johnson

If you've got 'em by the balls their heart and mind will follow.

Lyndon B. Johnson

After he became President, Johnson was once asked why he kept on J. Edgar Hoover as head of the FBI. Johnson replied:

Better to have him in the tent pissing out than out of the tent pissing in.

For socialists, going to bed with the Liberals is like having oral sex with a shark.

Larry Zolf

I didn't think John Diefenbaker was a son of a bitch. I thought he was a prick.

John F. Kennedy

Under certain circumstances, profanity provides a relief denied even to prayer.

Mark Twain

Well, Teddy, I see you've changed your position on offshore drilling.

Howell Heflin
on a photo showing Edward Kennedy in a
compromising position with a woman in a boat at sea

YOUTH

I have something to say but I don't know what it is.

Paris graffito

They pick the rhetoric they want to hear right off the top of an issue and never finish reading to the bottom.

Martha Mitchell

In America, the young are always ready to give those who are older than themselves the full benefits of their inexperience.

Oscar Wilde

Like its politicians and its wars, society has the teenagers it deserves.

J.B. Priestley

We cannot always build the future for our youth, but we can build our youth for the future.

Franklin D. Roosevelt

In history it is always those with little learning who overthrow those with much learning. . . . When young people grasp a truth they are invincible and old people cannot compete with them.

Mao Tse-tung

Praise youth and it will prosper.

Irish proverb

ZEAL

Zeal, n.
A certain nervous disorder afflicting the young and inexperienced. A passion that goeth before a sprawl.

Ambrose Bierce

There is a holy, mistaken zeal in politics, as well as religion. By persuading others we convince ourselves.

Junius

Zeal is fit only for wise men, but it is found mostly in fools.

Thomas Fuller, D.D.

Zeal without knowledge is fire without light.

Thomas Fuller, D.D.

Zeal is very blind, or badly regulated, when it encroaches upon the rights of others.

Pasquier Quesnel

Violent zeal for truth hath an hundred to one odds to be either petulancy, ambition, or pride.

Jonathan Swift

Motives by excess reverse their very nature, and instead of exciting, stun and stupefy the mind.

Samuel Taylor Coleridge

There is no greater sign of a general decay of virtue in a nation, than a want of zeal in its inhabitants for the good of their country.

Joseph Addison

The zeal of friends it is that knocks me down, and not the hate of enemies.

J.C.F. Schiller

ZOOS

All they actually offer to the public in return for the taxes spent upon them is a form of idle and witless amusement, compared to which a visit to a penitentiary, or even to a State Legislature in session, is informing, stimulating and ennobling.

H.L. Mencken

Legislatures is kind of like animals in the zoo. You can't do anything about 'em . . . just stand and watch them anyhow.

Will Rogers

Things have not changed much in the last two centuries, as evidenced below.

TO THE ELECTORS OF CONNECTICUT,

GENERALLY—AND

TO THE ELECTORS OF NORWICH

PARTICULARLY

I am a man of extreme *modesty*, and have been so considered from my youth up. To *extemporaneously* proclaim my talents, would excite such crimson blushes upon my cheeks that my friends would fear I was affected with the *scarlet fever*. I therefore sit down in my garret to write my claims to public confidence. In relation to myself, I have to day made an important discovery. The public shall know it—(O! how I blush here alone, I am so modest.) I was in the Revolutionary War, & have been from that time till now regarded, (& that truly,) a thorough federalist ; but I, this morning as the clock was striking seven, found out that I was a *true Republican*, and that I always *had been* one—I now proclaim it. I do think that my political orthodoxy, my extensive influence, and my public services, ought to entitle me to your votes for some public office ; I therefore offer myself as a candidate for a Member of Congress. If my services are not wanted in that office, as I am not a proud man, and am willing to serve my country any way, I will consent to go to the General Assembly this Spring. You cant deny to a *good Democrat* this office, and I know the public good requires my services.

I promise you I'll do *darned* well—I'll curse the HARTFORD CONVENTION seven times a day, though I am totally ignorant of its object—I'll proclaim in the morning and in the evening that the honor we gained in the last war was infinite, though I have forgotten the whole except the battle of Stonington— I'll swear three times each day that if it had not been for the new Constitution, Connecticut would have sunk, though I never read it—I'll go to Caucus and keep up the honor of *our* side and *our* party—In short I'll be the quintessence of democracy itself—so much for my politics.

I'll sway the Legislature by the " might of my power," and lead them by the " majesty of my" *influence*—I'll dig the *Channel in the River Thames* so deep that Mr. Simms can enter his subterraneous world by *diving*—I'll erect *Dams across Quinebaug river* so high that you may stand upon the top and dip water from the clouds—I'll incorporate fifteen *new Banks* in this town, with a capital of five millions each— The Stockholders shall make 75 per cent on their investments—The money-borrowers shall be supplied with a $100 if they will give their note for 98, without any endorser—I'll exempt *Manufacturers* from taxes and give them a bounty equal to 6 per cent on their capital—I'll make *real estate* rise 200 per cent in value—I'll make business for 9000 *Mechanics*, and they shall make, clear gain, 300 dollars per month —I'll make the trade of the *Merchants* increase ten fold—O! no tongue can tell what wonders I'll do.

Though I never went to College, and never made a *long* speech in my life, yet I'll hit 'em a dab— I'll regain the long lost honor of my constituents, and will speak three hours and a half each day—I wish to be in the fashion, for I am a *fashionable* man—I therefore very *modestly* request you to vote for *me*— I live on the *western sod*, and cant see you every day. I therefore, here in my garret, beg of you to vote for me.—"Whatever King or Prince shall reign, I'll be the Vicar of Bray, sir." I pray you vote for me— All my friends are in favor of me, therefore vote for me!

Ichabod Ward.

Norwich, March 30, 1825.

FOR SALE OR TO LET,

A neat finished House, on the West side of the river in Chelsea.

Enquire of ICHABOD WARD

Ichabod Ward was never elected to any state or federal office.

Index